Strategic Information Systems Planning
Readings and Cases

Strategic Information Systems Planning

Readings and Cases

Gurpreet Dhillon, PhD

Virginia Commonwealth University, USA

Semantic Books

Published by Semantic Books
An imprint of *The Information Institute*
2020 Pennsylvania Avenue NW, Ste 904
Washington DC 20006, USA
publish@information-institute.org

Made and printed in USA
Typeset in Palatino
ISBN-13: 978-0615645636 (Semantic Books)
ISBN-10: 0615645631

To all my students,
Who inspired me,
Who challenged me,
Who argued with me,
Who had a discourse with me,
And appreciated what I had to offer.
You are the best!

CONTENTS

Acknowledgements   *13*

Preface   *xv*

1. Introduction   *19*

   Networks   21

   Strategic Alliances   23

   Outsourcing   25

   Case Example: IBM and Air Canada   29

      Shaping the future   *30*

      Change presents opportunity   *31*

      Understanding through engagement   *32*

      A commitment to innovation   *34*

2. IS Planning   *35*

   Conceptualizing about Business and IS Strategies   37

      Business strategy tools   *39*

      The Boston Square   *40*

      Implications for IS Strategies   *44*

   Competitive forces   51

      IT and Sustainable Competitive Advantage: fad or hype   *53*

      Why IT by itself fails to provide any advantage?   *55*

      Two Paradigms for Sustained Competitive Advantage   *56*

   The IS Planning Process   58

   Critical review of assumptions in IS planning   63

      The organization has a business strategy   *64*

      There is a distinction between an IS and business strategy   *65*

      IT is a source of competitive advantage   *65*

There are a class of information system called 'strategic IS'   65

The strategic applications of IT can be planned   66

The IS Planning process helps in organizational integration   66

Challenges for IS planning   67

The challenge of reviewing benefits   67

The challenge of managing business change   68

The challenge of assessing organizational competencies   69

3. New organizational forms   71

Structural challenges   71

Interdependence   74

Organizational Structures   75

Boundary-less Organizations   78

Learning Organizations   81

Reasons for Evolution   83

Managing evolving organizational forms   84

Support and Commitment from the Management   84

Inculcating cooperation and communication   85

Change agents and opinion leaders   85

Employee Involvement   86

Developing an innovative culture   87

Maintenance of the change implemented   87

Conclusion   88

4. IT Competence   89

Conceptualizing about IS/IT Competence   90

Implications for the Emerging Firm   95

Balancing "Do" and "Think"   98

IS/IT Applications   100

Competency Gap   101

Implications for the Emerging Firm   104

Filling the Gap: Hybrid Managers in the Emerging Firm   105

Allocating Scarce IS/IT Resources   106

Information System Sourcing Options   109

Final word   110

     Best Practice Guidelines for Emerging Firms   *111*

5. IT Implementation   *113*

The Desire for Change   114

The Problem   116

Alternatives   118

     Leave it alone   *118*

     Continuous improvement and workarounds   *120*

     Re-engineer the system   *121*

Modernization Failures   124

Considerations   125

     ROI   *125*

     Project Management   *128*

     The Need   *130*

     The Future   *131*

Conclusion   133

6. IT and Managerial Discretion   *135*

Introduction   136

Related Background   138

     What is Collaborative Information Sharing?   *138*

Theoretical Foundations   140

A model of Transparency   145

Conclusions   149

7. IS Innovation   *151*

Delivery of products and services   153

Service Type   156

Spotting an Innovation   158

    Examples of Incremental Innovations   *162*

    Examples of pioneering innovations   *163*

Leadership competencies and innovation   164

Summary   166

8. IT and Social Responsibility   **167**

Accessibility to technology   167

Property rights and ownership issues   169

Freedom of speech issues   171

Quality and reliability of information and systems   173

Aspects of a viable social responsibility program   175

    Socially responsible individual practice   *175*

    Ethical systems development   *176*

    Establishing responsibilities   *177*

    Instituting training programs   *180*

    End-users need a lesson in ethics   *181*

Conclusion   183

9. VITA - a muddled affair   **187**

The Executive Summary   187

Introduction & Background   189

Partnership Contract & Implementation Strategy   192

Summary of Corrective Action Plan (CAP)   200

The future of VITA / NG   207

The State's interest   209

    Governor A or Governor B   *210*

10. Nevada DMV - the genesis   **213**

Background   214

Phase I - Foundation Phase   *216*

Phase II- One Stop Customer Service   *217*

Phase III- Alternate Service Methods   *217*

Implementation   217

Training   *218*

Online   *219*

Problems   221

Conclusion   222

11. Spa Select IT Implementation   **225**

Current Situation   227

Business Plan Identification   229

Planning   231

Training   232

Implementation   234

Property Management System Interface   239

Conclusion   239

References   **243**

About the Author   **260**

Acknowledgements

I began thinking about Strategic Information Systems Planning when I joined the Cranfield School of Management. John Ward had asked me to lead an industry sponsored project on "IT and Change". From there emerged a report on Chaos Theory and Strategic Planning. Those modest beginning allowed me to develop the ideas and engage in numerous meaningful discussions with my students, people I worked with and several consulting assignments. I acknowledge all those "strategic planners" who came in my contact and allowed me to further refine my thoughts.

Several people have contributed to the text. Notable among these are former colleagues from Cranfield School of Management (UK), including Oscar Weiss, Joe Peppard and Peter Murray. Contributions of my former colleagues from University of Nevada Las Vegas (USA), particularly Doug Orton are dually acknowledged. Over the years several current and former students have helped shape the text. Contributions of and deliberations with these students, particularly those in my INFO 641 class at Virginia Commonwealth University (USA), are most sincerely acknowledged. I also acknowledge contributions of Francis Fabian and David Coss to parts of the chapters.

Preface

The story of SABRE and Apollo and the "battle" that ensued between American Airlines and United Airlines never gets told. SABRE became so successful that it made sense for American Airlines to spin it off as a separate entity. Apollo got reincarnated to what is today known as Galileo and is presently owned by Travelport. The story of SABRE and Apollo also illustrates how *strategic information systems plans* get formulated and implemented.

In the case of SABRE, a chance meeting between Brian Smith of IBM and CR Smith, President of American Airlines, led to conclude that IBMs project with the US Air Force at that time was exactly what American Airlines needed to handle their reservations. As a result between 1957 and 1960, $40 million were spend to develop the system. United on the other hand create a grandiose strategy to emulate the success of SABRE. Competition however came from European airlines, which found it difficult to compete in the market place. United spun off Apollo, which later acquired Galileo, the European response to Apollo.

For the past four decades the airline industry illustrates a number of *strategic information systems planning* issues – relative advantages of companies because of information technology and rationally planned strategies, strategic use of technology, innovation, business and change, the role of discretion in decision making, leadership – to name a few.

In the recent past we have seen newer technologies define strategic planning. One that stands out the most related to the *Netscape* vs. *Internet Explorer* war. Even though *Netscape* began with a 80% market share, they were squeezed out of the market place, partly through litigations, by Microsoft. Though having lost in court and drowned in the marketplace, *Netscape* developers open sourced their code. It was to later emerge as *Firefox*.

Today we are entering a new era in information systems strategic planning. In this era the boundaries of the firm are being redrawn an grandiose strategies are giving way to micro strategizing. Times have changed. And we are in the midst of schizoid incoherence. The only thing that is constant is *change* itself. There is no perfect way to mage technology in an ever changing world. Competence to understand the chaotic patterns will be the call of the day. May be there is that strange attractor that needs to be understood. Or, maybe it just depends on the nature of the organization and the specific context. Whatever it might be, there is a need to delve into various facets of *Strategic Information Systems Planning*.

This book is a collection of readings in *Strategic Information Systems Planning*. The topic areas represented cover a broad and eclectic subject matter. I hope that in totality his book will offer a comprehensive understanding of information systems related strategic planning issues.

Gurpreet Dhillon, PhD
Richmond, Virginia, USA

1. Introduction

The basic premise underlying Strategic Information Systems Planning (SISP) is a distinction between an *IS strategy* and an *IT strategy*. The IS strategy is demand oriented focusing on information and system requirements in meeting business objectives. These requirements are captured in terms of applications. The IT strategy, on the other hand, is supply oriented and concerned with specifying the technology to deliver these applications. Prescriptive approaches have been proposed to help in aligning these IS/IT strategies with an organization's business direction through identifying applications which support the business and at the same time give direction to IT investments.

However, the central role played by the business strategy in defining the IS strategy and ultimately in determining IT investments must be called into question when descriptive evidence clearly indicates that strategy is emergent (Mintzberg and Waters, 1985), often serendipitous (Hamel and Prahalad, 1995) and continually changing. The irony is that in order to develop IT-based applications, business requirements must be clearly articulated and remain relatively stable while a technical solutions is being developed.

However, IT is changing at blinding speeds. As IT changes, so does the role that IT plays within organizations. Moreover, as new information technologies emerge, new organizational forms of business emerge as well in order to exploit these new technological advances and become not only more efficient, but also more flexible in hopes of gaining a competitive advantage. IT substantially changes the relationship between customers and suppliers, allowing it to become much more intimate because it enables this the transfer of important information across organizational boundaries.

In conjunction with the rapidly changing world of IT, organizations seem to be in a constant state of "schizoid incoherence," or constant state of change. In fact, advances in information and communication technologies have created a borderless world. Consequently, firms have had to learn to be extremely responsive to this borderless world around them and furthermore, IT has altered the way in which businesses manage their supply chain and has become an incentive to come up with new approaches for managing logistics across organizations. In order to take advantage of this state, businesses have become much more open to the formation of different types of cooperative networks or other types of organizational forms that can quickly and securely exchange important information. In many cases, sharing information through these organizational connections can increase a competitive advantage.

In forming these cohesive organizational networks, the relationships of the supplier/customer changes drastically. New types of environments are created in which there is interdependency between the organizations. The agreements that bind these organizations are not on word only, but are action related so that the success of one partner is a function of how well information is communicated and managed by the other partner or partners as well as how interrelated the connections are with other organizations. This creates an incentive to not only work effectively together, but also motivates companies to be extremely efficient in maximizing the strengths of each firm within the network.

In this chapter we consider SISP behind the backdrop of different organizational forms. IT facilitates the creation of new organizational forms, but the emergent structures recreate innovative use of technology. Overall, all these new organizational forms between different independent companies will lead to a higher level of competitive performance, only if they enable higher levels of operational benefits in the relationships between the parties involved. Furthermore, any success of new organizational forms is a function of how effectively coordination is realized through the use of IT.

Networks

A network form of an organization is one which is joined by particular groups of people, objects and events. There are two aspects that characterize a network:

1. A network is formed through the combination of certain elements

2. The elements within a network have specific relationships.

There are distinct names for different types of networks as well. There are loosely coupled networks and co-operative networks, which change dynamically to gain advantage in a marketplace. The competitive nature of such networks allows organizations to concentrate on their core competency, or focus on whatever they do best as a business. These core competencies are crucial to their existence and competitive advantage in the market. However, their competitiveness is reinforced and even enhanced by the connections that they form with other companies who can then help them in the areas in which they are less competitive or simply do not have the time or budget to focus on a particular area that is less critical to them. As other companies also focus on their core competency, the network grows and, more importantly, gains value as they obtain economies of scope.

IT plays an important role to create the network structure, and creating the framework or foundation enables a company the opportunity to expand their cooperative behaviors among them. Although IT can produce the framework or infrastructure for all parties involved, by itself, it does not guarantee the success of the network. Members in the network have to create incentives or a reason for other members to share knowledge and expertise with each other.

Often the benefits gained from using IT in the network are unevenly distributed. In many instances, network leaders (often the buyer firm) retain the largest benefits. For example, the buyer to supplier network, in which Chrysler is linked up with all it suppliers, enables them to better compare prices and supplier offers and then chose the one which best fits their needs. That also may enable Chrysler to pressure its suppliers for lower prices. The supplier, other than the opportunity of being a part of the business, does not gain any real advantages from this network.

Taking this example a step further, in implementing just-in-time (JIT) delivery of products to automobile assemblers, suppliers in the network make significant changes to their own materials, procurement, manufacturing scheduling, and logistics processes. These changes are designed to provide them the capability to deliver to precise lot sizes (determined by the assembler's production plan) at very short and precise intervals before the components are required in auto assembly lines. These specialized investments generate significant benefits by streamlining a range of processes. As the JIT function increases, so does the dependency of the supplier on the buyer, as their supplied parts become more customized and the switchover costs to change to another buyer increase significantly. Therefore, these investments create incentives to maintain the supplier relationship for the auto assembler network, as they would have to forego the benefits (if they ceased the relationship) created by these hard to imitate, specialized investments made over time by the supplier.

Strategic Alliances

Another type of network is a strategic alliance. Strategic alliances can be defined as one where particular resources and skills are grouped to achieve a common goal for the partner organizations. Typically strategic alliances have three common features:

1. The intent is strategic rather than tactical

2. The focus is on achieving long term goals

3. Emphasis is on tight linkages amongst partners

Strategic alliance can take two forms - non-equity based and equity based. Equity alliances are ones where both parties maintain an independent ownership, such as distribution alliances, manufacturing alliances and R & D alliances. Equity strategic alliances are the ones where the two partners have a joint venture with each other. One of the major concerns in a strategic alliance is that there can be problems of trust, opportunism, and social control far more complicated than those encountered in simple dyadic affairs.

Steve Steinhilber, who at one time was Vice President of strategic alliances at Cisco (currently Vice President Industry Solutions), believes that strategic alliances allow each partner to focus on their core competencies while extending its products and services to new markets. Moreover, the partnerships provide a lower-risk approach to quickly reacting to the rapidly changing marketplace while minimizing capital investments. IS plays an important role for the success of strategic alliances, especially in the area of information sharing. In fact it has been argued that information sharing is one of the key success factors in the functioning of strategic alliances and enables supply chains to be agile in responding to competitive challenges Strategic partnerships are the most mature, valuable, and difficult type of these relationships. In this case, the partners have a broad understanding of each other's needs and visions, and share important values. Hence, a strategic alliance "ties each other's hands" and focuses on building a close relationship of mutual trust, respect, mutuality, with open information sharing, gain sharing, and concern for each others well-being. Because the partnership shares so much, it is adaptable to change and transcends tactical difficulties.

In this new organizational form structure, often companies start out with one form and transform to another. For example, in 1994 Air Canada outsourced their IT operation to IBM as a first step. In 2001, having implemented a successful outsource relationship with IBM, Air Canada then went a step further and announced a strategy partnership with IBM. This partnership between Air Canada and IBM was a seven-year, $1.4 billion strategic partnership to e-enable the airline, enhance customer service and develop future solutions. Air Canada expected to save approximately $200 million in IT costs over the term of the contract. As strategic business partners, IBM and Air Canada worked together pursuing new business opportunities in the areas of customer service and leading edge travel industry solutions. These jointly developed solutions were offered to other companies through a marketing alliance created between Air Canada and IBM. "We are entering into a strategic partnership with IBM which will go far beyond managing our computer systems and which, we expect, will set a new standard in the airline industry," said Air Canada's Calin Rovinescu, Executive

VP, Corporate Development & Strategy. Besides the IT operations, IBM also manages Air Canada's IT infrastructure, including application development and maintenance, 20,000 workstations, employee help desk services and network and server operations.

Outsourcing

Another new organizational form, whose popularity seems to have increased in the past few years, is outsourcing. This is where an organization starts purchasing a service that was previously internally provided. This definition can be expanded to; simply hiring another company to taking over and run a service it can perform better and more efficiently than the parent company. In general, companies outsource activities that provide parity in the marketplace. Strategic activities are typically keep in house.

The top two areas for outsourcing in an organization are IT and HR services, due to the fact that at first glance, the cost savings seem to substantial. Herb Kelleher co-founder of Southwest Airlines simply puts it, "people who are in the business full-time can do it better and cheaper." Essentially, outsourcing has helped corporate America become more efficient, flexible and nimble. The logical perception is that companies that provide outsourcing should be the experts in the area for the service that they provide and should be able to offer better and more efficient services than an average company, which has their core-competence in other areas.

In April 2002, CIO Magazine surveyed 179 IT professionals whose companies outsourced their IT services. The results of this survey showed that the key factors for companies to outsource their IT services were lack of internal staff and the need to reduce IT costs. One such company, that is a good example of having a lack of internal staff, was Palm Inc, which was spin off in 1999 from its parent company 3Com. Palm's Vice President and CIO

Marina Levinson said in 1999, "we were a three billion dollar company growing at 100% a year and we needed to build internal capabilities fast." As a result, Palm outsourced 90% of its IT infrastructure. The survey also offered more detailed reasons for an organization to outsource IT, which includes: 32% of organizations have lack of internal staff, 29% of the companies were looking for costs savings, while 20% of organization wanted that quality of the IT services to improve. More recently companies have been outsourcing to bring in new capabilities. As is evidenced in the case of Virginia Information Technology Agency (see case in this book), outsourcing helped restructure the Commonwealth of Virginia IT infrastructure.

One issue of enormous importance, in order to create a successful outsourcing effort, is to create a good relationship between the organizations and outsourcing providers. The scope of the relationship between the service provider and the customer needs to reflect the fact that in business, like other aspects of life, nothing remains static. The service requirements laid out on the first day may be vastly different to those prescribed after three years of being in this partnership.

Furthermore, a long-term outsourcing contract is, by its very nature, uncertain. This is because a lengthy relationship will inevitably develop and change in response to the service requirements of the customer. The contract needs to address this uncertainty, but before this can happen, both the customer and supplier must ensure that they understand the shared aims and objectives involved. This shared understanding relies on forging a real partnership, supported by a good balance of risks and rewards. Many of the problems associated with long-term outsourcing relationships are caused during the process of reaching the agreement. The motivations of a person seeking to sell an outsourcing service differ vastly from those seeking to deliver it, and a long-term relationship between the provider and receiver will only prosper if the alignment is right. There is little hope of achieving this healthy relationship if the people who agree to the contract terms have no direct personal responsibility for its successful delivery. Drafting a contract with those issues in mind can be time-consuming and expensive, but it often proves to be an extremely worthwhile investment. Still, groundwork and planning can help to reassure both sides that all the important issues have been covered. In addition, it is not unusual for a long-term outsourcing project to take three to six months to finalize. Moreover, for an outsourcing partnership to succeed, IT professionals stress the need for a partnership that is equitable to both parties and one that is based on trust and mutual dependence.

There are various issues that need to be addressed with respect to risks associated with outsourcing of IT. The most common contributing factors to the failure of outsourcing relationships include:

1) often, pricing and service levels for outsourcing are established at the start of the contract; which usually contain no meaningful mechanisms for continuous improvement.

2) differences in buyer and supplier cultures often cause misunderstanding and distrust. Even if the cultures are compatible, the two parties still have fundamentally different goals and objectives that are frequently difficult to harmonize.

One example where cultural differences lead to the failure of an outsourcing relationship is Kodak. Although the company is seen as a pioneer of outsourcing, and was one of the first major U.S. firms to successfully outsource part of its information service department to IBM in 1989, its outsourcing relationship with Digital Equipment Corporation was not so glorious. In the same year, Kodak outsourced its voice networks to DEC. The computer maker's high-flying entrepreneurial culture and less-than-formal management style clashed with Kodak's buttoned-downed culture and management style. Ultimately the outsourcing partnership ended.

Other issues to be addressed include outsourcing contracts, which are based on key assumptions regarding technologies, business conditions, personnel, and other relevant issues. As soon as the contract is signed, these assumptions begin to change, and may lead to very different results and expected. However detailed the contract or favorable the terms, most contracts cannot anticipate the changes in an evolving environment. This phenomenon tends to ensure that at least one (if not both) of the parties will become disenchanted with the relationship. Longer-term contracts that lack flexibility tend to increase the likelihood of dissatisfaction. This is evidenced in the VITA-Northrop Grumman outsourcing relationship, which included as a case in this book.

Likewise, many buyers do not believe they have to spend any time at their outsourced operation, which is a mistake. Buyers frequently underestimate the time and attention required to manage an outsourcing relationship, or worse, they hand over the management responsibility to the vendor. The outsourcer begins to operate in a priority vacuum, and service levels tend to deteriorate because the outsourcer's agenda is not in sync with the buyer's business objectives. Another problem is a lack of management oversight, which normally is the result of two factors: first, the team that negotiated the contract often does not stay engaged in contract management and secondly, the new team, that may or may not understand the contract's intentions, is given responsibility for managing the relationship. Employees that understood the pre-outsourced environment have been transferred to the outsourcer's team. This disruption in continuity can have significant adverse effects on the outsourcing relationship. All these issues can enormously and negatively affect the outsourcing process.

Other than planning and choosing the outsource partner carefully, there are two other pieces of advice to companies considering outsourcing that could help to partially overcome some of the disadvantages experienced, especially due to false expectations. First, before getting into an outsourcing program, a company should consider where and why others have failed. Secondly, outsourcers are prone to sell more than they can achieve. There seems to be a case for both sides of the argument that points to the need for the organization seeking to outsource, to choose their partners carefully. A close examination of their methods and installation programs, to ensure it is as deliverable as they say it is, is suggested as a must. Penalty and get-out clauses have also been suggested as an area that needs consideration. It appears as though the outsourcing strategy is one that is here to stay; outsourcing is clearly a plus for those companies seeking a competitive advantage.

Case Example: IBM and Air Canada[1]

It's Monday morning in Montréal. As he does most every week, Patrice Ouellette has convened a coffee klatch with the small, energetic and tight-knit team he leads. While the mood is light, the agenda is all business. As Director of Customer Solutions and Innovations for Air Canada, Ouellette's mission is to keep a laser focus on improving the customer experience for passengers at every point in their journey. Known within Air Canada as the "Innovation Team," the group Ouellette has pulled together over four years has evolved into a well-oiled machine that is constantly attuned to which programs are working, which aren't and which processes can be done better.

When Ouellette calls himself and his team "data-driven," the description is apt, for data is the oxygen that fuels and directs the Innovation Team's efforts. At any time, he can get an accurate and

[1] Extracted from http://www.ibm.com/smarterplanet/us/en/leadership/ aircanada/assets/pdf/AirCanada_Paper.pdf

up-to-date read on how many people are using each of Air Canada's multiple self-service channels, what the trends are over time and what each check-in costs on a unit basis. At a basic level, this visibility provides Ouellette—as well as Air Canada's senior management—with a gauge of the business value and success of the company's self-service initiatives and, as such, a rationale for making future investments.

Shaping the future

While calling the perspective gained critical, Ouellette sees an even bigger value in the way such information can provide a roadmap for shaping processes, practices and even the layout of the airport going forward. For instance, when Air Canada's CFO asked Ouellette to put together a comprehensive analysis of the impact of four years' worth of self-service initiatives, the results reaffirmed the prevailing view that they were reducing costs, increasing revenue and satisfaction, and making Air Canada a stronger competitor. But the exercise also triggered the airline's Real Estate and Airports divisions to work together in managing the layout of its check-in facilities, changing the flow of passengers and—in the long run—reconfiguring or removing counters.

The path Air Canada took in becoming an industry leader in self-service is dotted with significant achievements. It started with Air Canada's kiosk strategy, through which the company led the industry in deploying "off-site" kiosks at different points in the travel ecosystem, beginning with hotels and eventually considering other possibilities such as car rentals, convention centers and airport- bound train stations—just about any place that travelers gather. It continued with Web-based check-in. Most recently, Air Canada broke ground with the delivery of a mobile self-service solution, first as an Apple iPhone®/iPod® touch application ("App"), then as a BlackBerry® App—in both cases a first among North American airlines.

From the all-important customer perspective, the Air Canada App is accessed simply through a single icon, which serves as a gateway to a broader array of information and services, including the ability to book flights, download electronic boarding passes, check in, get flight status and book rental cars and other services. Behind the scenes—and in keeping with Air Canada's strategic architecture vision—the solution leverages the same SOA infrastructure as Air Canada's other self-service channels, including the same set of common enterprise-wide services (such as flight status check). The efficiency that comes from this level of reuse is a big reason Air Canada was able to cut by more than half the time and cost required to bring the mobile solution to market (more on the benefits later).

Change presents opportunity

While the core mission of Ouellette's group—to continually look for ways to simplify the customer experience—has remained consistent over its four-year history, its practices have steadily matured. And while the group faced skepticism at the outset, a long string of successes has given Ouellette the credibility he needs to continue to push for change when the opportunity presents itself. As Ouellette points out, these opportunities often originate from the need to adapt to external—and sometimes event-driven—industry forces. "The airline industry is a very dynamic world, with regulations around security always changing," he says, citing the 2009 "underwear bomber" incident in the United States as an example. "While we're under constant pressure to reinvent the way we operate, it also gives us a chance to assess whether we can do something totally differently. So if new security requires us to add a new step in the check-in process, we ask: Can we streamline or eliminate other steps to make it simpler for the customer? That's the kind of dynamic that drives our change efforts."

The success of Air Canada's self-service transformation efforts also owes a lot to having the right governance framework in place, one that balances the fresh "outsider's" perspective of the company's change agents (i.e., Ouellette and his team) with the pressing day-to-day realities each of the airline's operational areas face in moving passengers and staying on schedule. This give-and-take process occurs within a group of stakeholders known as Customer Service Platforms, whose key members include IT, Airports and the Customer Service Organization. Meetings conducted monthly (or as events dictate) in a roundtable format are a mix of decision making, brainstorming and status review. One scenario may have the Airports Team presenting a new check-in requirement, the Customer Service team addressing how to inform customers of the change and IT figuring out how to implement it. Ouellette's role in this scenario would be to probe for how to yield a simpler process from the new requirement.

Under another scenario, it's the Innovation Team's job to inject new ideas into the mix and move them forward by proposing pilot solutions and working to get them implemented and tested quickly. Ouellette believes that to succeed in this role—an impetus for change—maintaining a degree of organizational separation from the rest of the business is a must. "We need people who instinctively and passionately think outside the box—who know the airline's day-to-day ways of doing business, but are not stuck in it," says Ouellette. "It's important [for the Innovation Team] to think from a different perspective and to keep asking why."

Understanding through engagement

At the time Air Canada decides to enable a new self-service capability, the Innovation Team's role is, in many ways, just beginning. Take a recent example, when Ouellette's team opted to develop a proof of concept for a new service, known as Paid Upgrade, and to roll out a test version on Air Canada's Web check-in site. Using its analytical tool set, the team was able to get an instant snapshot of who was using it and who wasn't. Further enriching the picture was real-time feedback from users and a usage analysis that pinpointed areas in the user experience where customers were more vulnerable to errors or misunderstandings. "It's a hands-on, highly engaged approach designed to get the best possible understanding of our customers," explains Ouellette. Just how hands-on? Ouellette regularly dispatches his staff to airports to observe with their own eyes the nuances of how people use Air Canada's self-service systems—and, most importantly, to learn from these insights.

So what became of Paid Upgrade? From the start, it showed unmistakable signs of being a major hit among customers. As Ouellette recounts, one influential blog writer endorsed the new service, lauding it for being "so easy, it took 60 seconds to do the entire process" and to get upgraded.

"That's the kind of impact our team gets paid to achieve," says Ouellette. Based on feedback such as this, the service was quickly expanded to include Air Canada's kiosk channel, and is now one of the company's most popular self-service features. Looking at the success of Air Canada's self- service initiative more broadly, the numbers speak for themselves. By moving passengers from counter check-in to Web, kiosk and mobile device check-in, Air Canada has produced efficiency improvements in the neighborhood of 80 percent for those transactions.

What makes Air Canada stand out isn't the fact that it's doing self-service, but the way it's doing it. By creating a common technological framework to underpin all of its self-service initiatives, Air Canada is able to provide a wider range of channels—and choices—to meet its customers' diverse preferences, and in doing so, drive a larger share of its customers to self-service channels. This enables Air Canada to not only reduce the overall cost of serving its customers, but also serve them better. That's because self-service frees up service resources to focus them where the human touch is needed, such as assisting children, the elderly and groups of travelers. Air Canada views the ability to provide this level of service as one more area where it can stand apart.

A commitment to innovation

For all Air Canada's progress in customer self-service, Patrice Ouellette considers it still in an early stage in its innovation journey. "We see our commitment to constantly elevating the quality of our customers' overall travel experience as the basis for our current success, and even more so as the foundation of our future," says Ouellette. "With its experience, technology, and knowledge of the business model, IBM has been critical to helping us meet this commitment to our customers."

2. IS Planning

Until very recently, and perhaps to some extent even today, IS managers would groan on hearing the phrase 'strategic planning'. This was largely because most would be busy dealing with legacy system problems, understanding the changing technology or gearing up to become 'e' enabled. There were also pressures to cut costs or to be in a position to have successful implementation. Any call for strategic planning would result in increased resistance and be considered a shear waste of time. Although many discount the importance of IS planning, it is nevertheless important when significant change is on the horizon. It may be integrating the Bank of America and Nations Bank computer system following the merger, or the implementation of a computer-based system for the London ambulance, careful thought needs to go into the process and various contextual drivers.

IS planning, simply put, defines a portfolio of computer based applications that will help the company achieve its business goals. In order to develop a plan that would really work, clearly the CEO and CIO of the company need to come together and discuss various issues. If this happens, an organization is in a position to create a well-integrated business and IS strategy. This is opposed to merely stating, "We need to buy more PCs" or "Lets buy Oracle" or "Lets have a web presence". It is well worth communicating and assessing what the needs are and how various systems and applications fit in with existing infrastructure and the overall business strategy.

At times a company may create a well defined plan that may fit well with the business strategy, but there may be problems of culturally aligning the IS plan with the organization. A new computer-based system might change the way people do things or super cede a particular persons authority. A new system may also impose too rigid a work environment, while in the past people would come together and do things informally. All these are cultural challenges that need to be considered, if IS plans are to be successful.

Clearly developing a good IS plan is a key to the success of IS in organizations. This chapter focuses on concepts and tools that that will help in undertaking successful IS planning. However some of the key issues that need to be addressed in order to gain success in planning include:

•   There needs to be a close alignment between the IS goals and the business strategy. This is possible when an IS plan goes beyond detailed system architectures and focuses on business benefits.

•   Senior executive buy-in is essential for a successful IS plan. This is possible only when the IS plan helps the bottom line.

•   A proper cost-benefit analysis should be an integral part of an IS plan. Intangible costs and intangible benefits are as important as the tangibles. There should clearly be options to improve and update the plan.

• The person responsible for developing and subsequently implementing an IS plan should be carefully chosen. Although it may be likely that a technology enthusiast close to drawing the specification may become the driver, it is only on rare occasion that such an individual may appreciate the business side.

In presenting material for this chapter we will logically classify the concepts into two parts. The first part will evaluate aspects of business strategies and the implications there might be for IS planning. Part two will focus on the process and tools and techniques available for undertaking IS planning.

Conceptualizing about Business and IS Strategies

Clearly business strategies are needed when a firm wants to identify a direction it intends taking. The nature of the business strategy however is a function of the complexity of the environment (see table 1). In a relatively simple context merely meeting the budget would suffice. Such exercises are carried out internally in the organization and there is an emphasis to reduce almost everything to a financial problem However if there is need to predict the future, to say determine demand for a certain product, then some sort of forecast-based planning would be essential. This would involve establishing multi-year budgets, undertaking a gap analysis and perhaps allocating resources in accordance with the gaps identified. In forecast based planning a number of external parameters are considered, including economic and market research data. Based on the data, sales and market growth opportunities are calculated and their impact on income and expenses assessed.

There may also be a situation, most likely because of competitive pressures, that a firm may be forced to think strategically. Such a case would warrant situation analysis, evaluation of strategic options and a dynamic allocation of resources. The company might want to reconsider the market it currently operates in and may decide to reorient based on competitive forces. In yet other cases, a firm may use certain opportunities to create a whole new market. This would need a well-defined strategic framework and widespread organizational capability to think strategically. Good example of creating a new market can be found in the online brokerage firms like E*Trade and Ameritrade that ushered in a new concept of stock market trading. Companies that create a new market or a different context are faced with another challenge. They have to continuously innovate in order to stay abreast.

Table 2.1, Classes of business strategies (in part based on Gluck, Kaufmann, Walleck, 1980).

	Nature of business strategy	Key activities
Class 1	Meet the budget	Focus on meeting the annual budgets Optimize internal functioning
Class 2	Forecast the future	Consider past performance and develop multi year budgets Undertake a gap analysis Consider allocation of resources to fill the gap
Class 3	Strategic orientation	Understand the situation Evaluate options Allocate resources for achieving strategic advantage
Class 4	Transform and create a new future	Undertake work in an innovative manner Well defined strategic framework Well established business processes

Classification of business strategies into four classes (table 2.1), affords some interesting observations and implications for IS planning. Clearly there are a number of situations where the business strategies and IS plans are not in sink. While an organization may be attempting to transform and create a new future, and many a times IS forms an integral part of the process, yet IS plans and strategies are considered in as class 1 or 2 activities. Consider the *Information Management* vision developed by Xerox. While the organization was attempting to transform the way in which internal information services were rendered, it considered IS as a cost and managed the technology resources as one would typically deal with class 2 projects. As a consequence, the mission of the organization and even the outsourcing deal with EDS where at odd purposes with each other.

During the late 1980s and early 1990s a general recession had forced firms to focus on the short term. This meant that any strategic project that would perhaps deliver benefits after a say two years was shelved. Companies wanted a shorter turnaround in order to justify the investment. This obviously forced many organizations to class 1 or 2. A similar phenomenon has been witnessed during early 2000s, essentially because of a recessionary environment. While the late 1990s saw a flamboyant economy, and companies ventured in to transform their businesses, the early 2000s because of lack of confidence in the market following demise of Enron and WorldCom, have been careful in their technology investment plans. IS has therefore been placed on the back-burner and at best investments are being made that would bring in efficiency of current operations rather than transform the organizational processes for some future benefit realization.

Business strategy tools

In order to deal with class 1 and 2 business strategies, there are numerous economics and financial tools that come in handy. In such situations IS are merely a means to bring about efficiency. Discussion of such tools is beyond the scope of this chapter. However for strategies that are classified as 3 and 4, numerous tools and techniques have been developed that help in conceptualizing and realizing the business strategy. The different tools help in evaluating a particular dimension of the problem rather than present a generic overview. There obviously are a number of implications for each aspect of the tool. In the discussion below, we shall discuss two business strategy frameworks that have had a profound impact on strategy formulation and implementation. These are:

- The Boston Square developed by Boston Consulting Group

- Competitive forces framework proposed by Michael Porter

The Boston Square

The Boston Square essentially brings together two concepts - product life cycle and relationship between market share and profitability. The product life cycle concept maps the demand for a product against time and identified four stages - initiation, growth, maturity and decline (see figure 2.1).

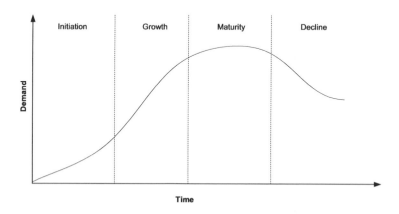

Figure 2.1, Product life cycle

The underlying argument in the product life cycle concept is that irrespective of the kind of a product, it generally goes through four stages. Unless an organization is in a position to identify the systematic position of its product in each of the stages and charts a future course of action, it will be difficult for that company to compete. Take the example of *Iomega* zip disks. When the product was first launched, it took the company a few years to become a standard in storage media world. The 100 MB capacity disks were a real bonus to computer users who could take back up and move large files from one computer to the other. However other players were taking market share away from *Iomega - viz.* cheap alternatives in writable CDs and other high capacity storage media. In response *Imogea* launched the 250 MB drives and disks with backward compatibility. This allowed the company to extend its product life cycle. *Imoega* was successful since it not only recognized the external threats, but also understood that their 100 MB technology had reached maturity.

Related to the product life cycle is the concept that relates market growth with market share. Given different combinations of market growth and market share, four scenarios are possible. First, although market share might be low, potential market growth is high. This situation represents a situation, where a new product is being developed and it is anticipated that the market growth will be good, but obviously current market share is low. Such products are 'Wild Cats'. From a strategy point of view, we are never sure what direction such products will move in.

Second, in a situation where market share is high and the market growth is also high. In such situations there is obviously a lot of potential in the product or service being offered. These are our 'Stars'. Major revenues are sought from the 'Stars'. Businesses however need to be aware that competitors are going to catch up. Stars roughly correspond to the maturity stage of the product life cycle. Unless a company has ongoing research and development to 'create' more 'Stars', its market share and market growth is going to gradually dwindle. A good example of this case is the development of the drug *Prozac* by Eli Lilli. For the six months ended 6/30/02, net sales fell 9% to $5.34 billion. Net income fell 21% to $1.29 billion. These revenues reflect lower *Prozac* sales due to the August 2001 introduction of generic competition in the U.S. market. In the pharmaceutical industry, for every 10,000 compounds that might be considered as a potential drug candidate, only one or two might make it through the development and approval stages. It is anticipated that it takes approximately $500 million over 10 to 15 years to develop a successful new drug. Although Eli Lilly was aware that its patent rights on *Prozac* were for a limited time, yet after spending nearly $2 billion annually on research and development the company was unable to create another 'Star'.

After a product remains a 'Star' for a while, competition takes over. This is the stage that marks the maturity of a product. Market growth for a given products slows down and while market share still remains high. Such products and services are termed as 'Cash cows'. It will perhaps make little sense to pump in extra funds into 'Cash Cows', since they are never going to become or 'Stars'. Significant research and development would be needed. In rare cases where the brand has significant recognition, it is possible to make some improvements to elongate the growth phase of a product life cycle (c.f. the introduction of 250 MB *Imoega* drives).

Somewhere along the way 'Cash Cows' become 'Dogs'. This is when the market share significantly declines and so does the market growth. A very good example of 'Dogs' can be found in many of the products in the automobile industry. In July 2002 Ford announced that the Excursion Sports Utility Vehicle would be discontinued from 2004 onwards. It was anticipated that the Ford would sell 50,000 Excursions every year. However being able to average at about 15,000 only, it became a 'Dog' relative to the Chevrolet Suburban, which was a 'Star'.

The above concepts are diagrammatically represented in figure 2.2. The product portfolio model emphasizes a few key issues in business strategy. These are:

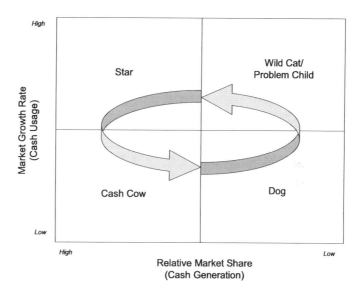

Figure 2.2, Product Portfolio

The product portfolio is a useful tool to begin thinking about a range of strategy issues. It emphasizes the need to manage products according to pressures in the market rather than internal factors. Implicitly it also suggests that net cash flows need to be diverted back into future product development. This will ensure future business success. There is also a need to have a well balanced portfolio. Over emphasis in one category may be detrimental to ongoing success of a product or service.

There are also a number of inherent weaknesses with the product portfolio. Clearly it is important to be aware of these if the product portfolio is to be used with confidence. One of the implicit assumptions of the portfolio model is that higher rates of profit are directly related to a larger market share. With respect to larger products, such as aircrafts by Boeing, there are usually high development costs that need to be taken into account. The product portfolio is normally applied to Strategic Business Units. It however needs to be noted that Strategic Business Units are business areas, not necessarily products. One might also end up assuming that there is going to be cooperation among various units. In reality however this may not happen.

Implications for IS Strategies

Since the strategies for a product will be different for initiation, growth, maturity and declining stages, so would be the strategies and plans for IS. If a given product is in the low market share and high market growth category, success is going to come from a series of innovations leading to a clearly focused niche. In such a case the relevant IS strategy option is going to be in enabling the creation of such a niche. This strategy was evidenced by *Amazon.com* when the company first entered the market. Clearly there was an extremely low market for selling books online, yet the prospects of market growth were rather high. Innovative use of technology enabled *Amazon.com* to establish itself over a period of time. However since cash generated was low and cash used relatively high, very quickly *Amazon.com* ended up in a problematic situation. Since *Amazon.com* had to keep the investors and venture capitalists at bay, they were forced to diversify into selling a range of other products through their online store.

If a product falls in the strong market and high growth or attractive market category, the implication is that the product will play a leading role for the company. The impetus for IS will be towards customer orientation and ensuring sufficient revenue growth enabling a 'star' performance. Systems supporting products in this category help in handling greater volumes more effectively and also ensure good customer relationships. There are numerous examples of products and services that have come into being in this category. Over the years such products and services have not only defined and established new markets, but have also radically changed the way in which business has been conducted. In the 1970s and 1980s, American Airlines use of IT to tie together the operational side of the business in a common information stream and then extending it to tie together the business side of American, resulted in giving American Airline a significant advantage in the marketplace. InterAAct, as the resulting system came to be called was one of the earlier system integration efforts in the airline industry. Coupled with the success of SABRE, American Airlines became well poised to thwart competition from other airlines.

In the late 1990s, Harrah's Entertainment was involved in establishing an electronic customer relationship management system, that helped in capitalizing on the low rollers in the casino industry. At the heart of Harrah's eCRM system was the Winners Information Network (WiNet), which was a centralized database to value of casino customers. As a result Harrah's has saved $20 million a year in overall costs, while increasing same-store sale growth. The number of customers playing at more than one Harrah's property has increased by 72 percent, and cross-market revenues have increased from $113 million to $250 million. It is estimated that $50 million of the 1999 profit of $594 million are a direct result of cross-market visits.

Implementation of an extensive real-time training system by 3M is another example of an innovative use of IS to remain competitive in the marketplace. In the fiber-to-desk cabling market where 3M has to compete with manufacturers such as Lucent Technologies and AMP, 3M created this system, which not only provides training but also offers significant marketing advantage by demonstrating the products to potential customers and enables self learning necessary to install the Volition Cabling System. 3M was able to develop this product since they had the comprehension that Web based training will remove barriers of time and distance and will continually provide easy access to customers and sales staff.

If a product is in a strong market position in a mature, lower growth market, it becomes extremely important to develop systems and IS support that defends the current position of the product or service. This is usually done by ensuring lower costs (or same as that of the competitors) and fulfilling demands in a most optimal manner. In this category, it's important to remain productive while controlling the customers and suppliers. Therefore systems tend to be oriented towards business control rather than innovation. Good examples come from the use of purchasing cards by companies in order to reduce invoice processing costs. The St. Louis-based agrochemical, Monsanto slashed its operating costs by issuing purchasing cards to its employees so they could pay for many non capital purchases. The company estimated that if a car is not used by the employees, it costs the company $40-$45 to process each transaction. By using the purchasing cards it has been possible for Monsanto to streamline its payment processes. Finally if the product is in a weak position (low growth or declining market), there is obviously going to be less corporate interest in it. Companies tend to begin thinking about disinvesting the product. Therefore IS investments for products and services in this category should really be based on the business intent and the direction the business strategy advocated. Innovative use of systems is uncalled for and will perhaps not be looked upon favorably. However in many cases companies are forced to keep offering a product or service, which can rightly so be termed as a 'dog', just because it makes sense to loose money (or subsidize) on one product or service for advantages elsewhere. For instance, it costs Microsoft and Yahoo! Money to sustain their free email services (see Box 2.1).

Following the product portfolio framework, researchers have proposed the IT application portfolio model (see Ward and Griffiths, 1996; Mc Farlan, 1984 as classic pieces of work). The IT portfolio defines the range of current and future applications. The applications could be *high potential, strategic, key operational* and *support*. The IT application portfolio is diagrammatically represented in figure 2.3.

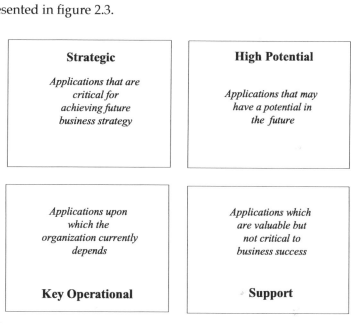

Figure 2.3, The IT application portfolio.

High potential IT applications. These are generally applications related to a new business idea or a technological opportunity that are realized through the development and rapid evaluation of prototypes. An inherent ability to reject failure is the key guiding principle. Hence the intent is to refrain from wasting any resources. Individual initiatives may be in one part of an organization and are generally owned by one individual who might champion them. Therefore an understanding of the potential of applications in relation to the business strategy and the likely economics is the key. High potential applications are founded on the assumption that they demonstrate value, which forms the basis of deciding whether and how these could be exploited. Allocation of specific responsibilities and mapping out the exact way to proceed is essential for realizing high potential opportunities.

Strategic IT applications. Strategic applications generally come into being because of market requirements and competitive pressures. Such pressures are more likely to be externally driven, perhaps from the suppliers and customers. Strategic applications therefore require a rapid development to meet the business objectives within a given window of opportunity. In case of strategic applications, the business objectives, success factors and the management vision to achieve them is pretty clear. It is also important to sustain the advantage achieved. Therefore an emphasis on flexible solutions that can be adapted to meet changing business environments is the preferred route. In case of strategic applications, it always makes sense to link the applications to associated business initiatives or changes to sustain the business commitment to IS development.

Key operational IT applications. Key operational IT applications are designed to improve the performance of existing activities in terms of speed, accuracy, effectiveness and economics. This is generally done by focusing on high quality solutions and effective data management. This ensures a degree of stability and reduced cost over a period of time. Key operational applications are largely founded on integrated systems, thus avoiding duplication and misinformation. Besides, risks because of inconsistencies are also minimized. This allows for balancing costs and benefits, which is so essential for an objective evaluation of alternatives.

Supportive IT applications. Support applications are founded on the principle of ensuring improved productivity and efficiency of existing tasks. Therefore low cost and long term solutions are sought. This often leads to selecting package software and at times compromising user needs because of solutions available.

Many support applications are put in place because of the legal requirements which have to be met. Support applications are changed or modified not for strategic gain, but to avoid obsolescence given the pace of the IT industry. Management of support applications demands the cost effective use of IS funds and resources.

Clearly applications in the portfolio evolve over time. At any given time a firm may have more than one high potential initiative. Given the market dynamics and the viability of certain applications, a few high potential applications may become strategic. When this happens, there is usually a loss of individual ownership. While it makes sense to tightly control the development and expenditures associated with a high potential applications, it is perhaps wise to let go of the control and seek senior management support of there is any hope of an application becoming strategic. If the senior management decides that there is value on the application, it becomes paramount fort he IT department to get involved with project. Issues time, cost and intent management become very important.

Over a period of time however strategic applications loose their luster. By now competitors may have either copied these applications or the market has just simply moved on. At this stage it becomes important to consider ways and means in which strategic systems could be fully integrated into the business processes. This helps in achieving effectiveness. Applications generally get re-engineered for long term use. There are occasions in the course of evolutions of applications that key operational systems need to be re-evaluated for the range of benefits and costs. Obviously lower cost options that meet the core needs are considered. There is a focus on standardization as well. Given the context of use, if it makes sense, key operational systems may result in being support applications.

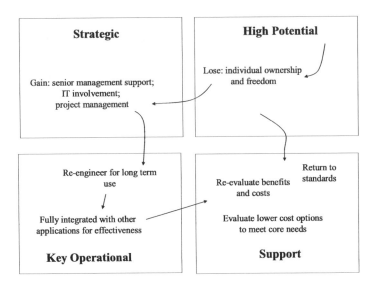

Figure 2.4, Evolution of applications over time (adapted from Ward and Griffiths, 1996).

Box 2.1: Sustaining free Email services

Hotmail: In 1998 when Microsoft bought Hotmail in a stock swap, the general consensus was that it got more than what it bargained for. Microsoft had inherited nearly 8.5 million customers and considered it as an ideal means to direct Microsoft products at them. The intent was to sustain Hotmail by selling advertising space. In 2002 Microsoft had some 110 million customers, however advertisements were covering a mere 20% of the cost. It is costing Microsoft about a $1 per year to maintain each mailbox. For this reason, the company is now focusing on generating non advertising revenues that can sustain the email.

Yahoo!: Nearly 80% of the Yahoo mail traffic ends up using other Yahoo services including stock quotes, news etc. The portal has always considered email to be the means to sell advertising. Matter of fact in the fourth quarter of 2002 advertising accounted for $189 million of Yahoo's revenue. However Yahoo! Mail has been money looser for the company. It is estimated that like Hotmail, even Yahoo! Mail advertising covers only 20% of its costs. Largely because of the dot com meltdown, advertising revenues at Yahoo plunged 35% in 2001 to $717 million

Other players: Smaller players like Terra Lycos and Mail.com have been having a real problem sustaining the business model. It is costing Mail.com (a unit of Net2Phone) as much as 6 cents to send each message, while the cost for Hotmail is about a penny. In terms of sustainability options are rather limited for these players. On February 19, 2001 AltaVista announced discontinuance of its email service and concentrate on the search engine and software businesses. For this reason, smaller players are trying new strategies. Mail.com for example is offering an ad free option for $19.95 a year. Other options being offered include POP access and mail forwarding.

(Based on reports in Business Week, New York Times and CIO)

Competitive forces

Michael Porter (1980) in his seminal work of competitive strategies suggests three generic competitive strategies for a firm. First is a *differentiated* strategy that relies on providing superior value. In this case products are difficult to imitate or replace with substitutes. Hence they command premium prices. Second is the *cost leader* strategy where a lower cost structure is advocated. This enables competition on the basis of price. Third is the *focused niche* strategy where a particular player finds a small specialty market. This is protected by geographic isolation and historically tight working relationships between buyers and sellers. Porter believes that these strategies form the basis of any successful overall business strategy. Porter, while discussing the competitive strategies, used an industry structure framework to determine appropriate strategies for a firm. In this framework he identifies five competitive forces: new entrants, suppliers, customers, substitute products, and competitors. Accordingly a good strategy should enable an organization to do one or more of the following: erect barriers against potential new entrants; change the balance of power in supplier relationship in favor of the firm; increase switching costs for customers; change the basis of competition among rivals in the firm's favor. These are illustrated in figure 5.

In a market place, one or more of the forces may be at play. There may be rivalry between existing competitors on price or aggressive advertising. The traditional competitors may also be cooperating with each other and forming alliances simply to thwart external pressures or threats. Suppliers and customers may form alliances with the firm so as to substantially increase the switching costs thus preventing other firms to be able to enter a marketplace. It may also be possible for new firms to enter a market place by virtue of a disruptive technology and hence be a threat to established products or services. It is also possible for innovative firms to develop substitute products and services and hence be able to create a totally new market.

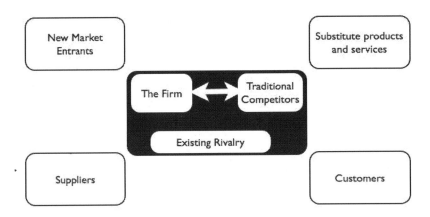

Figure 2.5, Competitive forces

Clearly if all the forces exert pressure at the same time, the business would indeed be in a dire situation. However if nature and scope of the forces is clearly understood and the potential impact adequately assessed, a firm would be suitably positioned to take on any competition. Technologies not only play a significant role in realizing some of the forces, but also in creating new forces. It is therefore important to understand the range of impacts of IS on competitive forces such that adequate strategies could be formulated.

More recently Porter has described how a firm's value chain can be used as a framework for identifying opportunities for competitive advantage. A firm's value activities are classified into two broad categories: primary and support. Primary activities are those that are involved in the physical creation of a product, its marketing and delivery to customers and after sale servicing. Support activities provide the inputs and infrastructure that allow the primary activities to take place. These are linked together to form a firm's value chain.

While discussing the role of IT in a firms' value chain, Porter and Millar (1985) argue that IT is permeating the value chain, thus transforming the way value activities are performed, besides affecting the nature of linkages among them. The competitive scope and the way products meet customer needs are also affected. Every value activity has both a physical and an information-processing component. Each activity creates and uses information. The role of IT is to enable a firm such that it can better co-ordinate its activities thus generating greater flexibility in deciding the breadth of its activities.

IT and Sustainable Competitive Advantage: fad or hype

It is argued that to create a sustainable advantage, one must either be blessed with competitors that have a restricted menu of options or be able to pre-empt them. This notion is further augmented by the research that illustrates competitive restrictions and unique factors such as macro-economic, political and regulatory, as having a potential to influence sustainability. Such restrictions can hamper a competitor from responding to a threat that it would otherwise answer. For instance, a company that is on the right side of public policy can exploit its position to build sustainability. This analysis on sustainability of competitive advantage can thus lead to a situation where the significance of the technological factor, needs to be explained in more realistic terms. As Clemons and Weber (1991) questions, "IT -equipment, and services- is available to all firms and most applications can be duplicated. To what extent can we duplicate successes, find critical opportunities, or even predict the effect of new venture?" Hence it may not be possible to gain and subsequently sustain advantage from the use of IT alone. Indeed there is growing skepticism among practitioners and academics suggesting that opportunities for achieving sustained competitive advantage from early use of IT may be more difficult than originally conceived and that the number of 'silver bullets' are few. Clearly some innovations are widely copied but their benefits can be defended; others are copied with no strategic gains for any player.

This means therefore that it becomes uncertain whether to rely on technology as being the enabler of gaining competitive advantage. For instance, Automatic Teller Machines (ATM) in banking are almost universally available and have produced no measurable benefits for most early providers. And an introduction of IT may be a 'strategic necessity' to maintain current competitive position. Therefore the competitive use of IT must be a component of overall business strategy; its application depends more on understanding unique business opportunities than competitive benefits achieved through technological features.

Why IT by itself fails to provide any advantage?

The proposition that technology can not be regarded as the only factor in gaining competitive advantage has been analyzed by many researchers. Cecil and Goldstein (1990), while discussing the predicaments of achieving sustainable advantage on the basis of technology, state that it is virtually impossible for major IT users (excluding vendors) to gain advantage based on IT alone. They suggest several reasons as to why information technology by itself fails to deliver a sustainable competitive edge:

- Peer competitors generally start with equivalent application knowledge: There may be differences after an application has been developed, but it's usually difficult to protect. Competitors can recruit key employees or use the same vendors and system integrators to take advantage of the leader's experience.

- Differences in IT developed capabilities among competitors can usually be evened out by vendors. For many applications, followers can purchase packages or hire systems integrators and end up with equivalent functionality at lower cost than the leaders.

- Larger scale rarely translates into a cost advantage. Larger companies generally have more complex requirements, increasing development costs. They are more likely to need (or think they need) customized systems instead of vendor-supplied packages.

Similarly Vitale (1986) suggests that attaining competitive advantage through IT may be difficult. This means that in many cases the initial innovator may, in fact, even place his firm in a disadvantageous position. Moreover the innovating firm can find itself in a week competitive position. This may be because:

- There are no first mover effects or barriers to imitation to give advantage to the innovation

- The innovation becomes a necessity and the innovating firm lacks special skill in producing this necessity

Indeed many applications of information technology are in fact strategic necessities. Such systems radically change cost structure, relative bargaining power, or the basis of competition to an extent where most competitors are compelled to imitate them. However, because competitors often imitate them or otherwise respond before customers change their behavior, these systems seldom confer competitive advantage.

Likewise, Johnston and Carrico (1988) argue that "virtually any corporation with a strong IS function can use the capabilities represented within that function as leverage to achieve improved competitive position in their industry". Therefore successful deployment is contingent to the presence of a set of external environment factors and in developing a set of internal capabilities that extend beyond the IT function.

Two Paradigms for Sustained Competitive Advantage

In the strategy literature there are two major paradigms for explaining sustained superior performance of the firm. The first of these paradigms draws upon the concept of industrial organization economics. Traditional industrial economics emphasizes barriers to competition, and takes the position that industry effects will explain the greater part of persistent above-normal returns. Particular industries are more or less attractive because they contain 'structural impediments to competitive forces' and thus allow participating firms to sustain competitive advantage.

The second paradigm for gaining competitive advantage of the firms suggests an alternative perspective - that firms are fundamentally idiosyncratic. Hence firms accumulate unique combinations of resources and abilities over time. These allow organizations to garner rents on the basis of distinctive competence.

The nature of firms' idiosyncratic endowments of proprietary assets as mentioned above has been further studied by. All competitive advantages are limited to a certain period. Firms develop idiosyncratic resources, which can be further deployed to achieve competitive advantage. It thus implies that the quest for new advantages is a critical responsibility. At the same time a need to understand the processes by which firms accumulate and deploy resources at the business unit level to effect superior performance within the industry, has also been emphasized. Hence processes used to develop new sources of advantage are as important to the vitality of a firm as the content of the advantage.

Thus the sustainability of the competitive advantage poses a major problem for strategists to manage the development of new sources of advantage to substitute the sources that are deemed unable to yield return. A principal mechanism through which organizations develop new competitive advantages is through the pursuit of new initiatives - attempts to add new products, markets and technologies to its current portfolio. Initiatives can lead to advantage in a number of ways. McGrath et al. describe these as:

- A firm may utilize resources, which are already at its disposal to tap new market areas, entering the new markets with lower cost, with greater efficiency or with more attractive offerings than competitors.

- The intention of the new initiative might be to contribute to the absorptive capacity of the firm. By entering small, less challenging markets initially in order to learn, it can develop product, market or technology assets.

- Firms are sometimes fortunate, gaining competitive advantage through luck.

By undertaking new initiatives firms can capture advantage. However two aspects must not be ignored in this respect: First, competitive advantage can hardly evolve from an initiative unless those responsible can develop competence at what they are doing. Second, competence should be thought of as a purposive combination of firm-specific assets (or resources) which enables it to accomplish a given task.

Competence of firm is the ability of the firm to reliably and consistently meet or exceed its objectives. An increasing convergence between the objectives of an initiative and its result has been regarded as a useful indicator of the potential advantage. For unless such convergence is occurring, it is difficult to argue that the team is developing competence, and without competence there can hardly be any advantage.

The IS Planning Process

IS Planning means the effective long term planning of IT applications in an organization. This section establishes the framework and process by which strategic IS planning can be undertaken. In order for IS planning to be successful, it is assumed that the process is closely aligned with business planning. It is also assumed that the outcomes of business planning will either inform or dynamically interact with the IS planning process. In organizational situations where there has been a limited exposure to IS planning it may be worthwhile to undertake an initial planning exercise in a few business area. This will help in fostering awareness and the importance of benefits delivery. There are however numerous barriers that hinder proper conceptualization and implementation of IS plans.

In research carried out by Basu *et al* (2002) it was shown, consistent with prior research, that insufficient senior management involvement was detrimental to the IS planning process. It was also found that excessive organizational and team commitment did not result in an adequately planned IS implementation. This was an interesting finding of this research and perhaps contradictory to previous research. It suggests that there is an optimal level of organizational commitment that results in IS planning success. The success of IS planning increases until it reaches a maximum, following which if there are increases in organizational commitment, success decreases. This finding is clearly consistent with traditional thinking that too much planning can have a negative impact on success.

Planning for IS is a cyclical and an iterative process. A number of frameworks have been proposed that help in undertaking IS planning. Martinez (1995) suggests that a significant amount of time should be devoted to creative thinking, which is followed by prototyping and experimentation. This sets the scene for design, development, implementation and rollout. A critical question that arises is as to how an organization will ensure creative thinking. It is important to ensure that the core of an IS plan is not constrained by the structured methodology. One effective means of ensuring creative thinking is to allocate substantial time to the thinking and avoid the use of any structured method. Prototypes may be developed, tested and later discarded once the purpose has been achieved. In due course as solutions begin to take shape, they need to be developed for actual business operations. This is the stage were effective project management and control techniques come to be used.

Creative thinking always plays an important role in IS planning . Since the very nature of IS projects is dynamic and new problems and situations arise at every stage, it is important to allocate sufficient resources to thinking about problems and potential solutions than dealing with situations in a reactive manner.

One of the major outcomes of IS planning is the development of a portfolio of IS applications. The application portfolio helps in realizing the business plans and in achieving the business goals. Organizations undertake IS planning to identify the right mix of applications in the portfolio. Typically applications are sought that provide higher payback, strategic significance and congruence with the organization's competitive needs. A long term view of IS planning suggests that the focus should be on improving organizational capabilities

Although the objectives of IS planning are generally well received, this does not mean that the adopted planning process is adequate. While some researchers have suggested a comprehensive rationally executed planning process, others suggest an incremental emergent process. Comprehensive planning is exhaustive and attempts to integrate a range of strategic decisions. Large groups of people from various organizational levels are involved in decision making. Extensive analysis is carried out. In order to manage a large planning group, some degree of formality is essential.

Critiques of comprehensive planning suggest that by focusing on formal planning methodologies and predefined criteria trivializes IS planning. This results in the IS planning exercise merely becoming a top-down activity. There are organizations however which do engage in incremental planning. In such cases the focus is on a limited number of themes and IS decisions are made on a one-by-one basis. Since the agenda is rather focused, it helps in keeping the team small, which in turns facilitates hight levels of informal communication. It often also becomes possible to experiment with new and innovative agendas. Table 2.2 summarizes the characteristics of comprehensive and incremental IS planning.

The Continuous Strategic Alignment model is perhaps the closest to the incremental method of IS planning. The model has five basic axioms:

- Governance processes specifying decision rights

- Technology capability processes specifying IT products and services needed to support business strategy

- Human capability processes specifying skills necessary to support business strategy

- Value management process that allocates resources to maximize IT investment benefits

- Strategic control that maintains internal consistency

Table 2.2, Comprehensive and incremental views of IS planning

Planning characteristics	Comprehensive practices	Incremental practices
Plan comprehensiveness	Plans are generally complicated and integrate with the business strategy	Simple plans that are loosely integrated with the overall strategy
Approach to analysis	Formal multiple levels of analysis are used to arrive at plans	Personal experiences and judgments are used
Planning organization	Planning is based on a formal representation from various groups	Planning is based on informal networks of a few key individuals
Basis for decision	Formal methods and criteria are the basis of decisions	Shared group understanding if a few key people forms the basis of decisions
Plan control	IS plans are periodically reviewed and are adapted to changing circumstance	IS plans are continuously reviewed and changed to adapt to the context.

The notion of strategic alignment and incremental planning is based on the theory that organizations learn and benefit by adapting to the context. However there has been criticism of incremental theories on grounds that they fail to address critical needs. Based on extensive research carried out in Netherlands and Finland, Salmela and Spilb (2002) propose the *four cycles method* of IS planning. The method divides the planning cycle into four distinct parts:

- Agreeing on planning objectives

- Aligning business objectives and information objectives

- Analyzing IS resources and IT infrastructure

- Authorizing actions

The difference of the *four cycle method* from the traditional comprehensive method is that inputs from techniques such as mind mapping are added to the process. Furthermore the four steps are repeatedly applied over a period of time. The repeated application ensures that the existing strategies are monitored and updated periodically. The first cycle begins with an assessment of progress in implementing IS decisions and plans. New issues that require attention are also considered. If immediate action is required on any issue, then a special task force is set up. The second cycle begins with a review of current issues. Progress in implementing IS decisions and plans is reviewed. The main purpose of the second cycle is to undertake strategic thinking. Innovations in the planning process are considered and various business and IS plans integrated. There is an emphasis on identifying those IS projects that add value the business strategy.

The third cycle begins with considering the progress to date. Specific attention is given to issues related to infrastructure planning, evaluating and establishing the organizational structure and development of a project portfolio. The fourth cycle focuses on establishing clear proposals for action. The intent is to ensure commitment of resources and mechanisms of acquiring such resources. Specific planning activities considered relate to identifying organizational implications; defining criteria for decision-making; authorizing final decisions. The *four cycles method* is illustrated in figure 2.6.

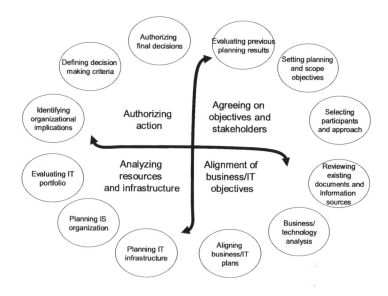

Figure 2.6, The four cycle model (Salmela and Spilb, 2002)

Critical review of assumptions in IS planning

In the previous sections we have reviewed some of the predominant methods for conceptualizing about strategy and means of undertaking planning. Over the years the variety of theoretical frameworks proposed have incorporated both business driven and creative approaches in the search for significant opportunities for gaining benefits from IT. These have included 'top down', 'middle out', 'eclectic' and 'multiple' methods. Incorporated within these approaches are a variety of tools and techniques, borrowed primarily from the business strategy area, including critical success factor analysis, SWOT analysis, five forces analysis and value chain analysis.

However, research and experience questions whether IS Planning in its many guises is actually working. Recent US research, for example, has highlighted that only 24% of applications recommended for development via a formal IS planning process were ultimately developed as organizations needed to carry out further substantial analysis post planning. One study even went as far as to suggested that the whole process of IS planning may be a cosmetic exercise. This was conveyed as a type of informal social consequence of traditional systems analysis and design.

The IS Planning process is grounded in a number of fundamental assumptions and in the remainder of this section these are surfaced and their validity is assessed.

The organization has a business strategy

One of the major assumptions which underlies IS Planning is that there is a business strategy in existence; after all this is what the IS/IT strategy seeks to align itself with. We saw in the previous section that descriptive research has shown it to be sometimes emergent, often serendipitous and continually being renewed. This presents a challenge to IS Planning in that it must align itself to a moving target. The requirement is that IS/IT strategy must itself be dynamic. While it *may* be possible to articulate a flexible IS strategy, the paradox is that in order to develop an IT application a strong element of stability and predictability is required. In essence, we saw above that business strategy formulation involves an ability to articulate and capture a diverse, fluid and informal set or organizational characteristics which, to date, IT professionals regard as functional, quantifiable and certain. Cynically, one could argue that IS Planning represents the IT professionals' requirement for certainty in an uncertain world rather than to involve business managers *per se* in the process!

Paradoxically, the business strategy itself is often constrained by legacy IT systems, which represent that results of past strategies as articulated by the IS planning process. This restriction imposed by IT has led many companies to go down the outsourcing route in search of a more responsive IT capability. However, this practice is fraught with danger.

There is a distinction between an IS and business strategy

IS planning makes a clear distinction between a business strategy and an IS strategy. The message which this conveys is that IT is something which is bolted on and in some way is secondary to the business strategy. However, in many industries IT is often intrinsically linked to the success of the business, particularly in information intensive industries.

IT is a source of competitive advantage

One of the principle assumptions underlying IS planning is that IT can provide a source of competitive advantage. The reality is that IT has become a commodity and in many industries today you cannot exist let alone survive without IT. The clear evidence is that IT alone does not generate sustainable competitive advantage rather it is through the business changes which it facilitates or its ability to leverage organizational capabilities. Recent research suggests that only IT managerial skills are likely to be a source of sustainable competitive advantage. The implications of this analysis is that the search for IT-based sources of sustainable competitive advantage must focus less on IT, *per se*, and more on the process of organizing and managing IT within a firm.

There are a class of information system called 'strategic IS'

The phrase strategic information system is now common in the lexicon of management. These are the systems which are seen as giving the organization strategic advantage. In reality, strategic information systems are in fact a misnomer. The so called examples of strategic information systems in fact represent a significant *process capability* which the organization has harnessed through IT. It is the process capability which is strategic to the business not the IT.

The strategic applications of IT can be planned

By engaging in IS planning the underlying assumption is that the strategic application of IT can be planned. Clearly the focus should be on 'thinking' prior to any execution. Evidence however suggests otherwise. In an analysis of four of the most well known strategic IS, Baxter's ASAP, McKesson's Economost, American Airlines SABRE reservation system and the French videotex, Teletel, Ciborra (1994) concluded that they were not fully designed top-down or introduced in one shot; rather they were tried out through prototyping and tinkering. This corresponds to Earl's (1993) organizational perspective on IS planning. His research, further elaborated upon in Earl (1996) concludes that 'effective [IS] strategies often emerge through implementation'. Planning is about programming not discovering. It is about articulating a route map in the context of a defined strategy. This defined strategy is the result of creativity, innovation and foresight: of strategizing. This presents a contradiction of sorts in that organizations' engage in *planning* to develop an IS/IT *strategy*!

The IS Planning process helps in organizational integration

The irony of IS Planning is that its supply orientation, with a strong focus on applications, can result in organizational fragmentation: exactly what IS Planning seeks to move away from. The assumption is that integration takes place at the technology level. While this may be the case, it is not always so. The end result, however, is usually more often about co-ordinating what results rather than integration. The implication of lessons from business process re-engineering (BPR) suggests that a strong process perspective should be adopted before any IT implementation is undertaken.

Challenges for IS planning

The previous section questioned some generally held beliefs about IS planning. The discussion touched upon the confusion surrounding IS/IT strategy and IS/IT planning. In this section we take the argument further and review the primary challenges for IS planning. These challenges can be classified into three broad categories: reviewing benefits; managing business change; assessing organizational competencies.

The challenge of reviewing benefits

One of the key challenges to IS/IT planning relates to inability of the business to reap benefits from IT investment. Part of the blame has been attributed to the mismatch between business strategy and the IS planning processes. It has been argued that if these are at tandem with each other, then there is a huge risk of benefits not accruing from IT investments. Hence it may not be sufficient to merely install an IT application and hope for the savings. At the very least, some training will be required, and probably changes in tasks, roles and responsibilities. This calls for a coherent understanding of the business strategy that may demand an investment, the IT strategy which may determine the nature and type of the system and an IS planning process which establishes a link between the business strategy and the IT strategy.

In the literature, it has been suggested that benefits of IT are often not realized because investment is biased towards technology. This may occur because of inadequate attention being given to the management of change, organizational structures and culture. Indeed managing change enabled by IT is at least as important as bringing IT to the organization. Indeed the challenge of reviewing benefits is becoming increasingly significant primarily because of rapid changes in both the market place and the technology itself. Johnston and Yetton (1996) bring out another interesting issue regarding benefits management and business change. Their notion of fit and compatibility suggests that the IT configuration of an organization should match the organizational structures. Although the main focus of the paper is on integrating IT divisions during a merger, the concepts seem to be equally relevant within an organizational context. Similar arguments have been proposed by other researchers as well, particularly those who have focused on strategic alignment. Prominent among these is the work of Henderson and Venkatraman (1993).

The challenge of managing business change

Organizations today are experiencing significant change. These changes have been afforded not only by advances in technology but also because of a competitive marketplace. This has resulted in the management of IS/IT related change emerging as a significant challenge for IS/IT planning. Indeed when an IT system is implemented in an organization, what actually occurs is change ranging from small scale and localized to major changes in the conduct of business and even major organizational restructuring. Change is not always welcome and can make or break organizations. It can be exhilarating or frightening but always creates uncertainty. Practitioners report that success rate for IT and change initiatives is well below 50%. Indeed some say that it's as low as 20%.

Research on Strategic Information System investments by McGolpin (1996) showed that in successful investments, coherent change management approaches were an integral part of the projects. Such approaches were geared towards delivering business change and integrated business strategies with IT strategies. McGolpin found that more often than not, IS/IT was considered as a component of a business project and was the key enabler in delivering business changes. The research further found that less successful organizations were characterized by planning and implementation approaches that focused almost exclusively on the technology. Such projects did not address in detail the business change aspects of the solution.

The challenge of assessing organizational competencies

The changing business environment coupled with a drive for getting benefits from IS/IT investments has generated a new challenge for IS/IT planning - the challenge of assessing future organizational competencies. An innovating organizations superior understanding of the technological and business aspects increases the likelihood that it will introduce competitively significant enhancements and thus sustain its advantage, despite innovation by rivals. This is becoming a key challenge in terms of IS planning, especially because of the prevalent disconnect between the business strategies and IT strategies. In the literature this disconnect has been related to the lack of organizational competence. The inherent argument is that IT applications have the potential to lower costs or create differentiation across a wide array of activities that constitute firms value chain. When applications create a differential advantage, they affect the structural characteristics of the industry and become important to successful strategy and organizational performance.

Competence to exploit an IT opportunity is influenced by the prevailing management culture, experience, and satisfaction with IT. Beyond technological feasibility and customer demand, there must be an organizational infrastructure capable of developing and moving innovations to market quickly. The impetus to develop the IT application does not come through mere existence of firms technological strengths. Organizations at the same time need skills that can react effectively to changes in the business environment. An understanding of the potential strategic impact of IT and integration with business processes may lead to greater IT utilization, and hence the sustainability of competitive advantage. In essence a large number of factors can jointly shape an organizations propensity to utilize IT in its quest for sustainable competitive advantage. Among these, evolving business conditions, technical competence, consistent exploitation of opportunities can be regarded as the key components.

3. New organizational forms[*]

We are living in an age where information moves freely and with much ease. Advances in information and communication technologies have also resulted in a change in the way humans can interact and the capacity with which they can make decisions. This paradigm shift towards an information-intensive economy has resulted in corresponding changes in organizational forms. Many changes are already apparent, and much more would be seen coming in the near future.

Structural challenges

During earlier years when it was not so readily available, information was the privilege of a few. Hence, organizational decision-making capacity was restricted to a few individuals. Organizations were bureaucratic in nature and built upon a strict hierarchical structure. Decision making authority, therefore, was bestowed on a few individuals higher up in the hierarchy, and these individuals had the most access to information. While one

---

[*] Contributions by my students Jeffrey Chow, Angadbir Salaria and Issac Janak to this chapter are acknowledged.

may debate on the pros and cons of a hierarchical organizational structure, any other structure was simply not possible because of the lack of means of information availability and dissemination. And so for the sake of economic viability, all investment in the distribution of the information had to be focused on being made available to specific people in highest echelons of the organization. Such organizations, thus have a top-down authority, where instructions come down from top levels and are implemented down the pipeline through a chain of authority. Bureaucratic, hierarchical organizational forms are still prevalent in institutions such as military and governments. It is relevant to note that such institutions are also affected by the forces of information availability and being constrained in how much information can be allowed to be made readily available, have to follow a hierarchical model of governance.

With free flowing and readily available information, however, the dynamics of decision making changes. Technology has made the availability of information possible in today's age. While institutions such as governments and military have reasons to guard information and keep it undisclosed owing to the nature of their responsibilities, other institutions now have the possibility of making use of this technological means to make information available to its stakeholders. They can thus distribute the onus of decision making across the board into units not only smaller, but also more focused. This ability has several implications:

1. **Faster turn-around in responding to business environment changes:** With information being available at good pace, employees in an organization can be made more privy to the market changes and where their organization stands in the current market. Information allows for emergent patterns to be sensed more rapidly, and organizations can then respond to these changes. Since decision making is distributed to smaller autonomous units, a unit sensing a need to respond can cut through a lot of time that would otherwise have been spent to get

the information up the chain of hierarchy and then get back an approval to respond. Thus, we have a much faster turn-around time when it comes to sensing a need for business change and then implementing them.

2. Improved decision making: Since smaller, focused groups make decisions pertaining to their sphere of influence within an organization, the decisions tend to be more informed and effective. The decision makers now have direct and relevant skills pertaining to the problem areas and can hence operate more efficiently. Hence, organization as a whole is making improved decisions.

3. Lesser governance in terms of implementing decisions: As noted, improved decision making and faster turn-around time in implementing decisions is made possible due to empowered and autonomous smaller units within an organization. An obvious conclusion out of this is that we now also do away with the two way back and forth of communication up and down the chain of command in an otherwise hierarchical organization. Such organizations thus have more of a *flat structure* and are able to do away with a lot of time spent in putting in place rules and governance to help facilitate communication up and down the levels of the organization.

4. Innovation hubs: With focused groups in place and little governance to oversee them, the organization can turn its smaller units into innovation hubs by mixing their organization with the right culture. Governance and policies as such impede creativity. Right culture and lesser governance, among other factors, contributes to the environment conducive of innovation.

The above four points have immense positive impact for an organization looking to move to become more customer-centric. Organizations have now realized that in order to remain competitive, they need to be more customer-centric in their actions hence there is a need to act quickly to changing customer demands. And thus a flatter structure helps an organization achieve that ability.

However, one cannot deem the hierarchical structure completely obsolete. We have spoken so far about the aspect of organizational structure purely in relevance to availability and flow of information. There are other aspects that are important to the success of an organization such as the organization's vision, mission, goals and being able to stay focused and true to their goals. Flat structured organizations are *network-centric* in their form and thus comes the big challenge of interdependence.

Interdependence

Interdependence is perhaps the biggest challenge of a more flat, network-centric organization. An aspect of an interdependent system is that the result of a transaction between the systems is intertwined with the actions of various players involved. Although we have an organization distributed into more focused self-organization autonomous units capable of making their own decisions, actions taken by one unit can affect others in the network as also the whole organization as such. This can make the management of the network extremely complex.

At this point, it is important to note that an organization can allow itself to function in a networked form only if its work can be "modularized." With modularized, we mean that if the organization appears to be comprised of heterogeneous sections and a certain section of organization's work can be deemed as being a functional requirement with very specific and clear set of deliverables, then we can say that the organization has a modularized requirement. Such modularization is then more preferable for it allows for a focus to be developed around the function, and thus the internal efficiency, and the output of the function can be improved owing to the newly found focus. To elaborate using an example, suppose an organization deems that employee access to the corporate email over the internet is a functional requirement of the organization, then the job of fulfilling that requirement is a modularized one. It can be debatable for the company to implement technology to fulfill this requirement using internal employees, or external vendors. However, it can be stated with certainty that a modular functional requirement exists. And we make the case that the unit fulfilling this requirement should be given autonomy to implement its own strategies and decisions to best achieve its objectives. Since the deliverables are clearly laid out, any form of governance and rules will be nothing but an impediment to the unit's ability to achieve its objectives. And so the unit can exist as an independent entity in itself, forming part of the network that is the organization.

It is important to note that all work of the organization cannot be modularized. And if such absolute modularization cannot be achieved with clear deliverables not having been discerned, then flattening the structure completely may not be desirable for the reason of the complexity derived out of putting in place interdependent systems. And then managing the complexity becomes an unwanted overhead.

Organizational Structures

The complexity of organizations and the extent to which they are exposed globally have created a need to adapt to intricacies rather than lessen them. As the complexity of the external environment increased, the ability of traditional functionally structured organizations to adapt to new demands diminished. The cause of this diminished adaptability was not from an increase in complexity and change of environmental factors, nor the inability for an organization to create new strategies, but was due to the inability of organizations to carry out the newly developed strategies (Bartlett & Ghoshal, 1989). A reaction to these issues was the advent of the matrix organizational structure which allowed for some level of flexibility for organizations to better react to environmental changes and bolster product development. The matrix structure is a hybrid hierarchical model which engages resources both vertically and horizontally within the organization to allow for a "flexible integration and application of technologies from a variety of sources to the development of new products and markets" (Miles et. al., 2009).

This hybrid model is composed of attributes from both multidivisional, a structure in which a parent company owns a number of autonomously managed subsidiaries and unitary forms, where the organizational management is directly involved in strategy and operations, drawing qualities from each. Ideally, the matrix structure model exhibits the efficiency and specialization of unitary forms and the flexibility and focus on customer needs of the multidivisional form (Miles et. al., 2009). These benefits allow organizations which employ the matrix structure to focus on specific products and services while remaining flexible to environmental changes or shifts in the market.

While this model provides several benefits in allowing the organization to give specific attention to products and projects, it is not without drawbacks. Given the structure of the matrix model, it is often the case that a single individual will have two separate managers to report to, product manager, and the manager of the department for which they work. This structure may be seen in Figure 3.1. Though the matrix structure provides many benefits through its flexibility in uncertain environments, this drawback can make or break an organization if not implemented correctly.

Bartlett and Ghoshal (1989) identify the drawbacks as less of a structural issue with the methodology and more as a behavioral issue. They state, "the most successful companies are those where top executives recognize the need to manage the new environmental and competitive demands by focusing less on the quest for an ideal structure and more on developing the abilities, behavior, and performance of individual managers…" succeeding only when those managers "assigned to the new transnational and interdependent tasks understand the overall goals and are dedicated to achieving them" (pg. 145). It is easy for managers to fall into the hierarchical line of thinking and forget the added complexity of lateral reporting structures. Focusing on this thinking limits the scope of what the manager considers in making organizational decisions and can hinder the success of products and ultimately the company's ability to profit in markets.

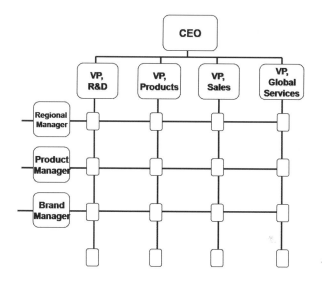

Figure 3.1, An example of a matrix structure.

Aside from behavioral change, other forms of matrix structures are available to organizations which may better mitigate the convoluted dual reporting situations which the matrix methodology creates. One such structure is the front/back hybrid matrix model which eliminates the dual reporting structure and streamlines the organizational hierarchy to prevent any convoluted management decisions or communications. The hybrid design is still of a similar matrix structure in that it provides integration of units within an organization; however, changes are made to the methodology behind this integration. In this model, the front end takes a strong customer focused orientation by providing integrated solutions, while the back-end contains the product business units which provide the individual components to be integrated into the solution. Although the front and back end still interact laterally, the employees within the organization either belong to one of the two sides, not reporting to both at one time.

IBM was one such organization which employed this model into its day to day business operations in order to better meet the needs of its customers. For IBM, it established its front end was organized by region and industry groups which were present in each region, and its back end which was organized into three groups, hardware, software, and services (Galbraith, 2010). While this structure is simplistic on paper, for IBM the structures of the organization were quite complex due to its size and expansion into other markets. According to Galbraith (2010), despite the organization's complexity, the front/back matrix structure enabled IBM to maintain "a stable set of common global business processes, a reconfigurable set of teams that are organized around the ever-changing portfolio of opportunities, and a reconfigurable set of decision forums for resolving conflicts and setting priorities (pg. 6).

Boundary-less Organizations

Jack Welch of GE was the first to coin the term boundary-less organization. Boundary-less organizations essentially remove traditional barriers between departments and barriers between the organization and external resources. Two models fall into this category: Modular Organizations and Strategic Alliances. Modular organizations aim to contract external organizations to complete all non-essential tasks. This model is one of the most flexible and can easily adapt to the needs of the market. The main organization does not have to spend as much time or resources to get to the level of expertise that the external organization already possesses. For example, a small software company may want to contract a marketing company rather than starting their own marketing department. The contracted company already has connections to the necessary resources and the knowledge to effectively perform the task. If the company was to start a new marketing department, qualified individuals have to be hired, and best practices adopted. The cost and required time to do so may be unsuitable for today's rapidly changing market.

Strategic alliances are the second form of the boundary-less model. This design emphasizes vertical integration by forming mutually beneficial relationships between two or more separate organizations. An example of this may be a business agreement to exchange trade secrets between say a cell phone and computer company. Doing so would allow both companies to gain insight about the other's specialty for a lower cost and shorter time. Perhaps the most beneficial aspect of this model is the conservative nature of the alliances. Since both companies are still separate, if one fails, the other may be relatively unaffected.

Similar to the matrix model, the modular organization and strategic alliances models also have disadvantages resulting from their structure. In a security context, opening up to another organization may lead to a myriad of different problems. If the organization does not have an effective existing security policy that requires third-party compliance, breaches and information leaks can occur relatively easily. Additionally, employees from other companies are usually not loyal to the primary company. Thus, they are less prone to offer suggestions, be proactive, or even fully comply with organizational policies. In order to have effective business partnerships, boundary-less organizations must spend a lot of time considering the possible structural or cultural clashes.

With the proliferation of the internet and globalization, organizations have spread internationally, increasing their size and complexity, generating a need for partnerships and interdependencies. Where an organization may have once been self-sufficient, companies must now depend on each other for support to each other's operations and successes. The shift to more complex organizations has created an inter-organizational environment of reliance and blurred lines of the organization's boundaries. The concept of boundary-less organizations is the definition for this type of organizational structure and may be found both formally and informally.

Formal types of boundary-less organizations include modular organizations, who outsource a number of functions to third-party organizations, and strategic alliances, which is a coupling of organizations who share similar strategic vision and have joined to expand their market and gain capital. These two formal organizational types serve separate purposes, each capable of uniquely benefiting an organization's needs. Where modular organizations might be of use is in technology industries where products are designed that incorporate a number of different components. An example of this would be the computer manufacturer, Dell, which incorporates a number of components designed and produced by other manufacturers such as Intel and AMD. Where Dell could incorporate production of components into their process, it is much more cost effective to utilize existing manufacturers and partner with them.

An example of a strategic alliance may be found in the partnership between Volvo and Dongfeng Motor Group of China. While this partnership may seem irregular, Volvo wished to strengthen their positioning as a heavy-duty truck manufacturer and sought to do so by aligning themselves strategically with Dongfeng. The alliance provides the two companies global reach and technological expertise of Volvo with the Chinese regional establishment and heavy-duty vehicle knowledge of Dongfeng to create a mutually beneficial partnership. Each of these types of boundary-less organizations supports the needs of organizations and have been especially helpful in contemporary markets as the complexity of technologies and products increase. The ability to partner with external organizations to achieve a similar goal allows for much greater flexibility and growth.

Finally, less formal organization which follows the same premise as other boundary-less organizations may be found in organizational interdependencies. In order for organizations to exist, let alone operate, they depend upon certain services which are provided from external sources. This interdependency between organizations forms a sort of an informal alliance through necessity. Data centers are often relied upon by businesses to provide storage of their critical IT systems, in order for their external networks and internal infrastructure to exist. These centers provide services but also depend upon access to transportation networks, service providers, and most importantly power infrastructure in order for their services to be operable. Without partnerships with organizations who provide these resources, even if by contract only, providers such as data centers would not be able to supply their necessary services. This notion places an increased emphasis upon the interconnectivity of organizations and their complex linkages and dependencies upon one another.

Learning Organizations

Although not an independent organizational form (must be used in unison with another model) learning organizations should receive some recognition. As previously discussed, the global market, especially in the technology sector, is growing rapidly. As complexity increases, employees need to keep up with current trends and developments. Learning organizations seek to address that issue by actively acquiring and applying new knowledge through experimentation with new technologies and analyzing current, previous, and future trends. Currently, many companies incentivize learning and proactive approaches to change. Bank of America offers a large variety of lectures, online tutorials, and telephone conference training courses available to employees and encourages employees to utilize these resources to their full potential. IBM setup failure toleration policies that encouraged risk taking in hopes of finding more efficient solutions and creating better products. In a world where companies are developing faster than ever, there is no space for complacency. Not only do companies have to surpass the competition, they must actively work to keep their competitive advantage through constant innovation.

As organizations have expanded internationally, greater demands for products and innovation have led to a frenzy of companies trying to find a competitive advantage and their niche in the market. This race to success has forced organizations to take risks in their path to developing the next innovative product that will propel them to the top of their industry. To assume that Apple developed their products without many failures and hardships beforehand is naïve at best. Companies who wish to achieve success in their business must employ some level of learning and risk taking strategy in order to develop competitive products and services. Antonoaie and Antonoaie (2010) describe such learning organizations as those who "typically seek to create learning climates that are characterized by experimentation, risk taking, collaborative inquiry, dialogue, and open sharing of feedback, expertise, knowledge and ideas" (pg. 105-106).

An example of a learning organization who employs these principles throughout their business model is Toyota. The method in which Toyota implements the learning organization methodology is through three steps. The first step is to identify the cause of problems with their products and develop solutions by asking the question "Why?" as many times as appropriate to delve into the most basic causes of issues. The second step for

Toyota is then to go through a period of self-reflection in order to identify means to improve and lastly, to leverage policy development through establishing high-level goals on the organizational level and implementing goals throughout the organization to support them. Learning organizations focus on self-improvement and internal evaluation. Learning organizations are encouraged to learn from their experiences whether positive or negative. Unlike Toyota, this model may be applied to allow an organization to evaluate and analyze not only their own successes and failures but the successes and failures of other companies from their industry.

Reasons for Evolution

As organizations develop, they eventually reach a plateau where their goals have been, for the most part, accomplished. At that point, they can choose to improve the product, expand into other areas, or stay the same. Staying the same allows for other competing companies to catch up, making it the least preferable of the three. Improving and expanding are the preferred options; however, they require specialized employees and innovative ideas. Specialized employees are few and innovative ideas can result in failure. As a result, many organizations try to develop their current employees into ones with specialized skills by encouraging them to take risks. Doing so would take out two birds with one stone, the organization gains more specialized employees, and new ideas will be generated and tested. The disadvantage to this method is the possibility for failure. The only way for this method to be successful is with an agile methodology where the organization fails quickly, gets back on its feet, and starts a new idea before others catchup. This is the primary reason traditional organizational models do not usually work in the modern age. Traditional models are too inflexible which is fine when things are going well; however, they do not respond well to failure. In matrix organizations, the failure of a team can result in that team being immediately assigned to a new but similar task.

Since teams are already created based on skill-set, there is less of a need to reevaluate the team. Additionally, since the team has already worked together before, it is no longer necessary to break the ice. Boundary-less organizations are quickly able to change by simply partnering with another organization after a failure.

Managing evolving organizational forms

Following are some factors that can be thought of as being major contributors to the success of evolving organizational forms:

Support and Commitment from the Management

This refers to the degree to which the top management, executive sponsors and important stakeholders support the change that is being introduced in the organization. Whether it is changed in the hierarchy of the organizational structure or the implementation of an IT project which is majorly technical, the support from management is a stark necessity. These changes need time, effort and funding. None of that can be invested if there is no constant and guidance from the management. Without the help of governance from the management, it is not feasible to manage or rather handle the change that is brought about. Employee resistance and budget overrides are the potential inhibitors during implementation of major IT changes in the organization. But they can be taken care of if the management provides commendable support. It is also important for the senior management to give some degree of autonomy to the middle-level managers in this direction. That is because, change inclusive of growth is only possible if management at all levels is supportive. The management needs to receive an accurate estimate of the time, resources and requirements of any planned project. The support from management, thus, is required from the beginning till the end of the implementation of any change brought about in the organization.

Inculcating cooperation and communication

Conveying the proper message is a skill not everyone can master. In a change that involves complex technology, it is not surprising to see that the employees get influenced by rumors and automatically develop a resistance and inhibitions towards the oncoming change. Informal communication among the employees is also very important as every rapport gives rise to some brainstorming. It is beneficial for the organizations to used methods like internal audits, special interest groups, workshops, and interactive sessions among employees to encourage cooperation. Also, by doing this, it can be ensured that all the employees will be on the same page with regard to the technological shift appearing in the organization. Another strength that is drawn upon by more interaction is the feedback that employees give each other. When the advice or suggestions come from colleagues at the same power hierarchy, the acceptance is usually high. Discussions of strengths, weaknesses, opportunities and threats among employees and bringing them to the notice of the top management will increase productivity as the involvement is high.

Hence it is non-negligible that effective communication and understanding among the organization's workforce is quintessential for any change that is brought about in the organization.

Change agents and opinion leaders

Change agents are those individuals or small groups who initiate, encourage, support and guide the employee base of an organization while the organization undergoes a major change. Quality managers are usually seen filling this role. They try to bridge the gaps in the process. They facilitate technical support, feedback, training, appreciative gestures for successes etc. They try to ensure that the organization does not remain in the schizoid incoherent state.

Opinion leaders are those individuals, either internal or external to the organization, who encourage and support the oncoming change in the organization. These could be project managers, engineers, members of a local government or anyone who acts as an advocate to the change that the organization needs brought about. They also help eliminate any kind of negative vibe coming from the employees regarding the transition. Many organizations are known to invite technology change champions from outside the organization so that the employees get a perspective that is new and other than that imposed by the management in the organization.

Employee Involvement

Activities that must take place for the organization to implement any technological change within itself should involve participation from the employees of the organization. The degree to which the employees participate in these important activities is called the employee involvement. Employee buy in is as important as or maybe even more important than the stakeholder buy in. This is because ultimately, in any organization, it is the employees who are the end users of the major technological change. If the employees are not comfortable with the deployment or usage of the new technology, the technology will not be used to its full potential.

Also it is important to ensure that the change is accepted by employees of all departments. If the focus of change is more external to the organization than internal, the employees feel that the perceived value by the management is less. This results in disinterest among the employees which in turn makes the whole change initiative useless. Also, if the employees feel that the importance given to one other department is more than that given to their own, it develops a hostile behavior. It is very important to balance the interests and awareness of all the employees of the organization. The employees must perceive themselves as belonging to the organization and the organization as belonging to them.

Developing an innovative culture

The cultural setting in an organization needs to be such that the human resource of the organization is active and accepts change easily and contributes to it. Innovation among employees is to be encouraged. This can be done by rewarding the employees who come up with new ideas. This gives incentive for the employees to be proactive and work for the benefits of the company. There are companies that encourage entrepreneurship wherein an innovative idea conceived by them, if meritorious, is adopted by the company under the leadership of the particular employee.

The company funds the project and ensures flow of resources. The success of such a project gives credentials to the employee in question. This encourages and inspires other employees in this direction. It is a mutually beneficial setup where both the organization and its employee contribute equally to the technological change in the organization. Since the efforts and capability of the employee are not overshadowed by the company, the employees put genuine effort to get recognition. This in turn cultivates a culture of innovation.

Maintenance of the change implemented

It so often happens in organizations that the changes brought about are not stably supported and maintained. If the desired objectives of the project are seen as the result of inculcating the changes, it takes time and effort from the management to ensure that the users are correctly utilizing the new technology or process on a regular basis. They need to provide continuous feedback and motivation to ensure the utilization of the new methods. It is not surprising that here will be problems, glitches and setbacks in any change initiatives but they need to be eliminated at the earliest with the involvement of the staff members.

Stabilization of the change only occurs when it is completely and welcomingly adopted by the employees and other end users. This new organizational form slowly develops into an old one, thus paving way for another new development. This cycle continues and organizations see dynamic changes regularly. The onus is upon the management to provide for the stabilization of the organization in light of technological changes that more often than not, meet with resistance both internally and externally.

Conclusion

It is difficult to conclusively decide on a "best" organizational form; however, matrix-learning organizations are generally the most stable. In house employees allow upper management to have greater control in terms of internal culture and policies and the use of project managers allows for far greater flexibility than the traditional functional design. Telecommuting is becoming increasingly popular, making it nearly impossible to use just a functional model. As projects become increasingly specialized, department managers cannot shoulder the entire burden of multiple projects. Project managers will be able to solve that problem. The learning aspect would enhance the organization's ability to quickly develop. Additionally, in-house employees are more loyal to the organization which directly impacts their willingness to suggest new solutions and perform outside of their normal duties. Traditional organizational forms may have worked in the past, but they have no place in the current age or the future. As markets and technologies change, so will business structures. Ultimately, successful businesses will be the ones to adapt quickly and efficiently.

4. IT Competence

What makes companies like Microsoft, Dell Computers and Apple so consistently successful? Moreover, how did they come to achieve such prominence in the marketplace when they started so very small? What were their first steps toward gaining a sustainable competitive advantage? What can a young emerging firm learn from their success to improve their own chances for success?

The evolutionary path to success is still somewhat of a mysterious phenomenon. Some would suggest that each of these firms has developed a core competency in their industry, but it seems that these companies have been quite successful even when venturing into new territory (AOL/Time Warner for example). Often success of this magnitude is attributed to the employees within the firm. While this may be true in part, there is also an undeniable competency that can be attributed to the organization itself apart from who ever sits at the firms' desk. Certainly, the companies have not achieved success overnight, but rather through a rapid evolutionary process of organizational learning.

Successful use of information technology has also played a large role in the success of these companies.

Recent MIS literature has suggested the notion that firms of this caliber possess several organizational competencies in various aspects of their business. They further suggest that firms must not only possess highly talented individuals but also have well-defined, established organizational processes in place. Their successful use of IT stems not just from being able to design and implement technology, but also from the ability to harness the benefits of that technology to yield tangible improvements for the business. These concepts and theories, which we will refer to collectively here as "organizational competence", have only begun to take shape by a few select authors over the past decade or so.

The idea of organizational competence is quite expansive. The scope of this chapter is limited to two primary areas. The first section will review the general theories and ideas regarding organizational competence that have evolved over the past decade. The second section will focus on a specific competency often overlooked by firms of all sizes: the ability to harness the benefits of information systems and exploit information technology to yield maximum value to the business. Each section begins with a discussion of literary concepts (generally targeted towards medium to large sized organizations). Then, those concepts will be applied and adapted for use within an emerging firm. The conclusion will offer a summary in the form of best practice guidelines. These guidelines are offered to managers of emerging firms to allow for very practical use of academic concepts tailored towards large established organizations.

Conceptualizing about IS/IT Competence

While the concept of core competencies has had more than its fair share of research, the concept of organizational competence has gone largely un-noted by the mainstream business community. However, there are a few researchers that have investigated the subject in sufficient depth. Because this topic is relatively new and not especially well researched, it is worth reviewing the general concepts as they apply to all firms.

Dhillon and Lambert (1996) stress the difference between organizational capability and organizational competency. Capability refers to a company's ability to create and sell its product in the marketplace. It is a high-level organizational concept and can be used to assess the company in its business environment. For example, one might ask, "Are they *capable* of doing such a project?" If the project is accepted, the capability of the company will be determined by the project's success or failure. Over time, the firm will be considered as having a certain level of capability based on the collective successes or failures of its ventures. Ultimately, the firm's existence rides upon whether or not it is capable of producing and selling its product.

A subset of organizational capability is organizational competence. This refers to the ability of an organization to properly deploy and manage its resources in order to produce a desired outcome. That outcome will then contribute to the firm's capability. In order to be *capable*, a company will need to be *competent* in several different areas of the business such as Marketing, Human Resources, Information Systems, and Technology to name a few. Thus competency is more of an inward-focused view that acts to serve the firm's ultimate goals in the external marketplace.

Literature in the area of competency falls within two primary categories: one that is focused primarily towards the skills of the individuals within a firm and the other that stresses the importance of the organizational processes of the firm. These elements work together to yield a certain competency level for the firm's divisions as well as for the firm overall. Organizational culture plays a strong role in an organization's competency. A firm's employees and its organizational processes constantly interact and affect, and are affected by, the company's culture.

Individual skills are the abilities of the people in a given organization. These skills include both company specific know-how as well as externally gained experience and knowledge. It is important for a firm to have a competency in obtaining human resources that not only meet the necessary skill requirements, but also compliment the culture of the firm and its business practices. Often times, this will happen naturally without any effort on the firm's part. This is due simply to the fact that applicants generally seek out companies with cultures that match their own personality type.

Managing organizational processes is much more of a challenge. Organizational processes include both formal procedures as well as informal practices. Formal processes tend to be well documented and relatively static. Because they are written out and easy to understand, high level managers often make the mistake of equating their organizational processes with their written policies and procedures. However, there is a very influential informal element that affects the firm's day-to-day practices. Over time, these practices, whether or not they agree with the policies and procedures, tend to have a strong affect on the organization's culture. Powerful factors such as tradition, culture, norms tend to overpower the formal written policies. It is a significant management challenge to balance the informal and formal ways of doing business.

Figure 4.1 offers a simplified example to demonstrate the interactive elements of organizational competency. This hypothetical organization creates websites for companies who wish to improve communication with their employees. Because the company is experienced in creating this type of product, there are several well-defined guidelines for the employees to follow. For example, the project team should first determine the client's requirements for the website. Next they would create mock-up pages (graphical prototypes) and present them to the client for approval before actually beginning the creation of the website. The design company will also need the skills of several different types of employees to complete the project. For instance, they will need authors and editors who understand the intended audience and purpose of the content they are creating. In addition they will need programmers versed in the relevant languages being used for the website. Together the individual skills of employees are utilized according the prescribed organizational processes to create a successful output.

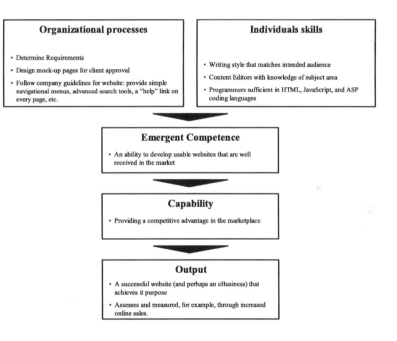

Figure 4.1, Elements of organizational competence (with examples)

As organizations evolve, a point of homeostasis is reached regarding the best mix between the required individual skills and the extent of organizational deftness. This mix will vary according to the contextual factors of the industry, company or divisions within a company. While there is no definitively correct ratio, we can typify the requirements that are generally found in different types of industries. Figure 4.2 offers a graphical representation of this. Note that the Y-axis represents the required level of individual skills while the X-axis represents how well defined the processes must be for the firm. For exemplary purposes, four categories of firms are shown. For example, organizations such as top consulting firms typically require both well-established processes as well as highly educated employees. Research and Development firms on the other hand find that when first developing new technologies, what is most important is having highly skilled scientists. Other firms, such as those with assembly line production, tend to require less skilled workers because they have created highly defined processes. Finally there are still some industries, such as those found in developing countries, which function with a relatively low-skilled employee base and do not have well-defined processes.

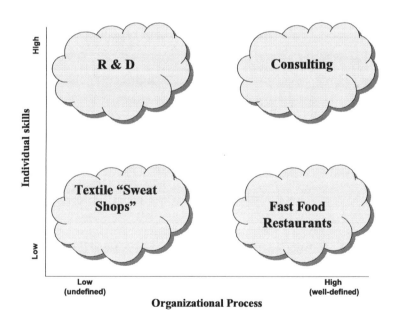

Figure 4.2, Categories of organizational competence

While Figure 4.2 is somewhat oversimplified and there are most certainly exceptions to the categories shown, it does point out an important principle: *Not all firms will demand the same mix of individual skills and defined organizational processes.* Understanding the context of an organization and the industry the internal and external environment is crucial to determining the best balance for a given firm. With this knowledge, a manager can work to improve the competence of the organization by allocating resources appropriately.

Implications for the Emerging Firm

The concepts discussed above can be useful to managers in understanding their organizational competence requirements. With this knowledge, they can begin to create strategies to plan and implement changes to improve the competency of their organization. However, the concepts are not readily useable within the context of an emerging firm environment. The emerging firm lacks the knowledge and experience that more mature firms have established. The idea of change management cannot exist in this environment because there is nothing to change from. Thus to offer value to managers of emerging firms, the concepts must focus on *creation* rather than change. Quite literally our interest is on that of Business Process *Engineering* rather than Business Process Re-Engineering, Process *Structuring* rather than Re-Structuring and *Defining* rather than Re-Defining the way the firm does its business.

There is an important concept regarding organizational processes in an emerging firm. When a firm is first conceived, its competency completely stems from individual skills. There are no organizational processes (formal or informal) defined for the firm. There are no policies, traditions, culture or norms. There is no relying on the typical established firm's crutch of "that's the way it's done around here". Some might even argue that by strict definition, there is no true "organization", only a group of individuals. So, from day one, the emerging firm manager must begin defining processes and methodologies that will lay the foundation for improved efficiency and organizational deftness. In simple terms, she must define "the way it's done around here".

Figure 4.3 demonstrates this graphically. We will assume that the small emerging organization consists of very highly skilled participants. Thus, the firm starts out at the point indicated by the red circle. As processes are defined, the organization begins to move to the right along the X-axis. This is shown by the arrow marked A, and demonstrates an increased level of definition in the organization's processes. As this occurs there is also an "invisible hand" effect that occurs. This causal effect (represented as Arrow B) occurs because less individual skill will be required once a particular process has been properly and accurately defined. The employee only needs to know how to follow the documented steps in order to complete a given task. The manager(s) is then free to move on to the next challenge. The end result for the emerging firm is a better utilization of resources. The firm is able to utilize lower skilled workers to perform a given task, while the highly skilled manager can further define organizational processes to increase the competency of the firm.

The two forces (Arrows A and B) combine to produce a shift in the elements that make up the organization's competency. The intensity and direction of the resulting shift will vary depending on the strength of forces A and B. The dotted arrows on Figure 4.3 indicate 3 possible scenarios. Arrow y represents a typical situation where increased process definition causes a moderate shift in the firm's requirements for individual skills. Arrow z would be an example where the definition of processes caused a relatively large impact on the firm's requirement for individual skills. This scenario would likely occur when the process at hand is easy to comprehend and highly repetitive, thus yielding itself well towards lower skilled individuals. On the other hand, if the task is very complex or highly varied, the individual skill requirement will not change significantly. This situation is demonstrated by Arrow x.

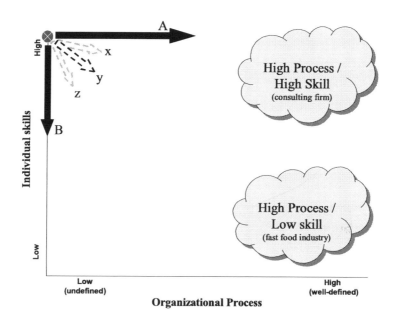

Figure 4.3, IT Competence in an emerging firm

While it is tempting for the manager to desire both highly skilled individuals and highly defined processes, she must consider the contextual situation. Specifically, she must consider the firm's mission and the industry it is involved in establishing processes. Is the firm destined to become a highly processed company with low skilled workers (such as the case with fast food restaurants)? Or is the start-up a consulting firm where both process and skill levels must be high? The answer should help the manager when choosing what level of effort and which processes should be defined and when. While there are certainly going to be many pragmatic elements to these decisions, this model should help prevent the over-utilization or under-utilization of resources towards defining its business processes.

Balancing "Do" and "Think"

To put these concepts to work on a day-to-day basis, the emerging firm manager can consider her efforts as being one of two types: "Think" and "Do". *Do* refers to the act of the manger simply performing tasks herself, requiring all of the manager's skills and little or no defined process. *Think* refers to the act of defining the process to perform a task. The manager's efforts to *think* allow the responsibility for the task to be handed to someone else in the organization, thus freeing up the manager to utilize her high skills in more appropriate areas. As time progresses the firm begins to take shape. It reaches a given competency level through a combination of individual skills and organizational process. While individual skills and organizational processes are not mutually exclusive there is a certain amount of give and take between the two, given scarce resources.

While a good manager's goals will revolve around defining methods and processes, there is an impetus that is constantly opposing this goal. This force stems from high internal and external demands to get things done immediately. Although the manager may understand the importance of proper planning, it may be a constant struggle to do so because other stakeholders in the organization often request the manager to primarily *do*, not *think*. While every employee in every sized firm certainly feels pressure to produce a tangible output in lieu of proper planning, the influence in a start-up is remarkably high. Oftentimes, start-ups are funded by outside investors and they tend to want to see continual progress. Phrases like "we need it yesterday" and "we'll have to organize the process later, for now we'll just do it ourselves" run rampant. In the typical start-up, there is an overwhelming amount of tasks that must be done. In addition, there are very few resources in which to do them. Whether the challenge faced is complex or simple, almost invariably the fastest and easiest way to accomplish it is by just doing it. However, this is short-term thinking.

Eventually if there is an overemphasis on doing at the expense of proper planning, it can and will lead to disaster for the manager and possibly even the entire firm. Typically the start-up manager's excuse for not planning is that even if a process were defined and documented, there would be no staff to carry it out. While this is perhaps true at that moment, we must assume that eventually the firm will have the resources. And therein lies the caveat. By following this line of thinking, the firm will be in a position where it is unable to achieve greater competency levels regardless of the amount of resources it has at its disposal. Thus, upon the first influx of large investment capital the company is paralyzed. It will find itself with plenty of resources for new staff and new technology but will not have the ability to use them. Because short-term thinking has caused a manger to *do* and not *think* in the first stages, the business processes are almost entirely ad hoc. In this situation, there is no way to utilize resources to improve efficiency until a huge effort is made to organize, define and document the processes of the business. Needless to say, for the capital investors, the idea of a very young firm having to re-vamp its operations is not very attractive.

As time progresses, the collective decisions made by the firm's actors begin to forge the firm's individual style and culture. This is an evolutionary process and, while it can be changed at any point in the firm's evolution, it becomes increasingly difficult to do. Norms that have been formerly or informally created over time become very strong and difficult to break. Thus it is in the manager's best interest to establish these norms properly from the very beginning. The start-up firm's elements of competency are more influenced by how the manager has faced the tasks before him–either by thinking or doing. Hopefully, the manager has made the right choices and led the evolution of the company toward having a high competency.

IS/IT Applications

An emerging firm that has invested proper resources towards "think" is in a much better position to begin considering the use of IT to automate some of its simpler tasks. While by no means revolutionary, the use of simple automating systems can drastically decrease the demand on the firm's resources to "do". There are often IT solutions available that can be readily implemented for these simple tasks with a high chance of success. A simple example might be utilizing an automatic timecard system to replace the need for someone to disperse and collect time sheets from employees and manually record employee hours. Implementing this type of system should be quite easy assuming diligent attention has been given to the process beforehand. In essence the timecard system has taken on the "do" element according to the process definition defined by the "thinking" of the manager. In the same light, had the timecard system been implemented within the very first day of the firm's existence, even this type of simple system would be much harder to implement. The failure would lie in the demand for the system to automate a process which has not yet been defined.

We can conclude that there is a direct relationship between the complexity of a task and the required amount of thinking that must be done to implement a successful system. Where only a minimal amount of thinking was required in the timecard system example, much more consideration would be required for a feature rich intranet system implemented to improve office efficiency. Because of the added number of variables and complexity, the system warrants much more advanced planning. Thus an increased amount of the firm's resources must shift towards thinking, should it choose to accept a more complex project.

Competency Gap

The logic of first planning then doing is quite powerful. For basic support systems (such as a timecard system) an emerging firm will generally find success by following the simple rules of think and do. However, technology has much more potential than mere automation. The ultimate goal for all sized firms is to implement IT systems that generate order of magnitude improvements for the firm. For the large firm, these complex systems can result in obtaining a competitive advantage in the marketplace. For the emerging firm, a successful strategic system can result in a true evolutionary step launching the firm into an established viable company. Conversely, we often find poor use of complex technology at the root of many failed start-up firms. For the emerging firm, a poorly executed strategic system will almost certainly result in the demise of the firm. While large firms tend to have the ability to "bounce back" from the losses caused by failed IT projects, emerging firms often do not have this financial luxury.

Firms of all sizes find much difficulty in their ability to harness the power of technology in order to improve their business competency. Despite great efforts in planning (i.e. thinking) and proper creation of a system (i.e. doing) the implementation can still result in failure. Rarely can the failure of the IS project be solely attributed to technical failure. Nor does the primary problem usually stem from a horribly misguided vision from the business leaders. Thus, we can conclude, there must be some other element that is necessary to implement large complex strategic IT systems. Quite literally, there is a gap between thinking and doing that is causing even the most diligent efforts to fail.

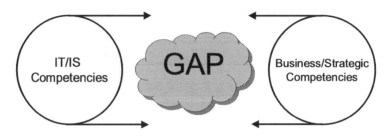

- Ability to create functioning technology
- Ability to maintain the systems

- Ability to lead firm in the most fruitful direction
- Ability know what is needed from the firm to excel

Figure 4.4, IT competence gap

The presence of this gap is unarguably real and contributes to the fact that nearly 80% of all large scale IT projects fail. Included in this statistic are the projects launched by the most highly rated companies in the world. Companies that otherwise demonstrate very high competencies in technology and business strategy repeatedly experience failure in their IT projects. Figure 4.4 shows the situation for a typical firm, regardless of size. This model is particularly effective in showing the primary source of problems for the typical firm: separation between the IT function and the business function of the firm. The IT department can build and maintain systems, while the strategists are experienced enough to understand the external market and understand internal environment dynamics. However, there is still a missing element. This element involves the need to coordinate these efforts and exploit the power of technology in ways that will support the strategy of the business. In essence the gap amounts to the firm's inability (or "lack of competency") to translate the strategic vision into functioning information systems.

A model developed in the literature that eloquently demonstrates three factors of organizational competence: Strategy, Supply and Exploitation. Each factor implies a specific role on the development of organizational competence. The role of Strategy (usually carried out at the executive level) includes monitoring the internal and external business environment and identifying key drivers that can be cultivated into opportunities to establish core competencies. Supply encompasses both the tangible and intangible resources of a firm, including the abilities of the individuals as well as the organization itself. This role is of a more operational nature in that it provides the resources necessary to add value to the firm's product(s). Finally, we reach the role of exploitation. This is where the use of properly aligned information systems can play a vital role in the success (or failure) of an organization. Thus the actors in this role are seeking new and innovative ways to harness the power of technology in hopes of improving the organization's competence (see Figure 4.5).

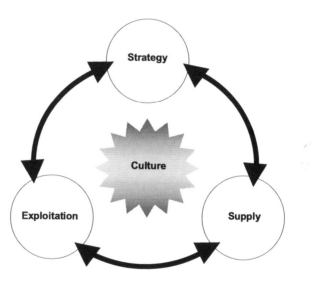

Figure 4.5, The competence wheel

To better understand the tertiary role of exploitation, we can draw an analogy to constructing a custom built home for a customer. The IS/IT group is similar to a team of construction workers. At the lowest level, their role is one of "doing". On the other side would be the creative designer. This role involves understanding the customers' wants and needs and deriving how the house can provide the most benefits to the owners. Their primary function is one of "thinking". Even with both of these roles being performed however, there is still a gap that will greatly impede the successful creation of the home. There are many required steps to be taken between "thinking" of an ideal home and "doing" the actual construction The construction industry is well aware of this, which is why several intermediary roles exist such as architects, technical designers, and housing developers to name a few. Essentially each of these roles involves progressively translating the general vision into specific "hammer-and-nail" instructions. The people in those intermediary roles are able to communicate effectively and understand with either side and thus facilitate the building of the house so that it is in accordance with the customers' wishes while still within the abilities of the construction crew and the bounds of economic feasibility.

The same basic philosophy equates to the construction of effective information systems. Even if a firm has exceptional business strategists and an IT staff with superior abilities and experience in building complex IT systems, an additional role is required. The responsibility of this role is to harness the competencies of both the business strategists and the information technologists to improve the competency of the business itself. In IS literature, this role is considered the role of exploitation. If done effectively, the firm can begin to harness the advantages of technology.

Implications for the Emerging Firm

Again, to bring these concepts to a more pragmatic level it is useful to place the concept of exploitation in simple terms that an emerging firm manager can readily use on a daily basis. In keeping with the concept of "think and do" we can illustrate the role of exploitation.

In essence, the IS/IT people are "doers". Of course they are also avid planners with respect to the design and creation of the technology itself. However, in the organizational context, their responsibility hinges upon "doing" (implementing the systems). The strategy people, on the other hand are considered the "thinkers". While not actually implementing a solution, they prescribe the benefits sought in order to remain competitive in the market. Thus we see the same gap as in the construction analogy. The IT people and the executive managers almost certainly will not be able to accomplish their collective and individual goals by working directly. Rather, another important role is necessary. We might call this activity "coordinate".

The long-term survival of an emerging firm depends on its ability to create and implement a strategic system to support its business goals. If implemented successfully, such a system can rapidly advance a firm's competency and possibly offer a strategic advantage in the marketplace. Likewise, due to the exorbitant amount of resources required to create such a system, failure can result in the termination of the firm. Thus when a firm is ready to consider a strategic system, it must be prepared to appropriate resources to all three of the roles: thinking, doing, and coordinating.

Filling the Gap: Hybrid Managers in the Emerging Firm

Providing resources specifically to exploitation in large firms often requires additional staff or even an additional management layer on the organizational hierarchy. This is often necessary particularly if the organization is either very large or its business and IT elements have drifted radically apart. However, given the size and age of the typical start-up, added staff may not be necessary in its earliest phases. This is not to imply that the role is any less important for the emerging firm. While communication problems may be less of an issue for a young firm, comprehension problems between the business element and the technical roles are evident in every firm regardless or size or age.

For an emerging firm a reasonable way to provide adequate efforts towards harnessing the benefits of technology is through the use one or more hybrid managers.

The term "hybrid manager" is defined by Michael Earl as:

"A person with strong technical skills and adequate business knowledge or vice versa...hybrids are people with technical skills able to work in user areas doing a line job, but adept at developing and implementing IT application ideas."

For a small firm with a juxtaposed skill set, the hybrid manager can help form a bridge of pragmatic understanding between the two parties. The effective hybrid manager is able to not only communicate effectively with businesspeople and technical staff, but can actually *understand* them to a certain degree. This does not mean the hybrid manager must be completely versed in both business strategy and technology, but she must understand their goals and their mindsets. Thus, they should have had at least some education (either formal or informal) or experience in both business as well as technology. This type of background will offer many benefits in both the comprehension of the subject matter as well as the social acceptance among both groups. Cultural acceptance is very important when negotiating with individuals or divisions. Ideally, the hybrid manager will not be considered "one of us" or "one of them" by either party.

Allocating Scarce IS/IT Resources

As discussed, the amount of effort put into the role of exploitation is directly related to the complexity of the system required. Since there will likely only be one or two managers which would fit into the hybrid role, it is very important for the manager to quickly discern what projects warrant or do not warrant attention. Just like established firms, the emerging firm must consider its portfolio of applications.

The importance of categorizing all system proposals is to discern the amount of resources (think, do, coordinate) that the project will demand. Systems are differentiated according to their potential contribution in two areas: business goals and performance objectives. Thus four categories of systems are derived: Support, Key Operational, Strategic, and High Potential. Support systems are generally basic, well established technologies such as simple task automation. Key operational systems are similar but slightly more advanced. These two systems will offer little or no strategic value to the emerging firm, but their effective use increase efficiency in day-to-day tasks. In contrast, Strategic systems are the "golden key" for the emerging firm. These are the systems that support the very core of the firm's business. For many start-ups, success absolutely depends on this category of systems. High Potential systems are typically experimental, high-risk projects. While they do offer the possibility of exponential returns, they also carry a high risk of failure. As such, they are not applicable to emerging firms and should not be attempted.

First and foremost, the hybrid manager should consider what benefit the system is supposed to provide. This is a crucial step when deciding where resources should be allocated. Future systems development can be categorized according to their potential benefits. If the benefits sought from the system are small, little resources should be used in the creation and implementation of the system. The start-up organization can afford no technological luxuries. Only systems with specific business benefits can even be considered. In addition, projects that do offer a particular benefit must be considered in light of other projects being pursued.

Figure 4.6 summarizes three types of systems. Each Venn diagram represents a different type of system. The size of the diagram indicates its level of required resources. The blue and gray circles represent the concepts of Do and Think respectively. These elements overlap to indicate the required role of coordination (exploitation). Note that strategic systems not only require a larger amount of "do" and "think" but they also require a greater proportion of coordination or "exploitation" efforts. However, long-term strategic benefits warrant the additional efforts.

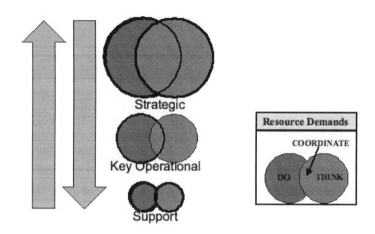

Figure 4.6, Types of system

While long-term success is the ultimate goal, the emerging firm manager cannot completely ignore short-term everyday technological needs. The suggestion here is not that the manager should hurriedly implement shoddy office support systems. This would eventually demand even more resources after the install and frustrate the businesspeople and the technical staff alike. The suggestion here is to limit the features of support and key operational systems as much as possible. The support systems, at least in the early stages, should provide only *needs* not wants. The caveat of providing unneeded functionality is that if it is regularly used, the users begin to rely on it as if it were necessary. In the event that the feature is necessary, it should be considered a key operational system and warrant more attention.

Information System Sourcing Options

Oftentimes, support systems can be achieved quite easily via packaged software applications. While probably not the perfect solution, these widely used applications can be very effective for simple IT solutions. In a typical emerging firm, employees will probably already be accustomed to using this type of industry standard software. This is of particular convenience to the manager because basic maintenance (such as installations and updates) can be performed by the individual employees themselves.

Key operational systems require slightly more resources from all parties. These systems may often be implemented by purchasing a software solution and customizing to suit the firm's needs. Thus it is important to determine what those needs are. While these systems become increasingly important to the support of daily activities they must not be allowed to demand excessive resources. Often, the requirements determination process for these systems is more a negotiation process. All employees must understand that increased effort towards this type of system will pull resources away from the firm's most critical system – the strategic system.

The Strategic system is by far the most important system for the emerging firm. It will often determine the fate of the company as a whole. Typically, this system should be created in-house, however, depending on the type of business the emerging firm does, outsourcing can be an option if it is a first tier agreement and is managed very carefully. Oftentimes, an emerging firm can outsource or purchase individual modules and incorporate them into the custom strategic system. Furthermore, the focus must be on systems that will provide an eventual competitive advantage and even a barrier to entry for inevitable copycat firms that arise following the successful rise of a new firm. As a rule of thumb, the firm's portfolio of applications should allow for 80% of the manager's resources to be allotted to this type of system.

The focus of the emerging firm's IS/IT resources should always remain on the strategic system(s). The company literally depends upon this system's ability to support the firm's aspiring business. Lower level operational and support systems must be kept as basic as possible. Any added features, no matter how easy to implement, will increase the system's complexity and demand increased maintenance and technical support. However, keeping the demands of fellow employees on lower level systems is not always easy to do, particularly in a small office environment. Often the support systems such as the office intranet and LAN are what the businesspeople in the office use on a daily basis. Consequently, they will tend to find much room for improvement in such systems. In addition, most of those employees have likely come to the startup from established corporate environments, and have become accustomed feature-rich IT support systems. It is important that the emerging firm's IS manager make it clear that additional features will detract from the focus towards the strategic system. Again, the rule of thumb applies and allows for approximately 20% of the firm's technical resources go towards basic functional support systems, leaving the remaining 80% to focus on the long-term strategic system(s).

Final word

The concepts and theories of proper IS implementation apply to all firms. Regardless of size, a successful company is highly dependent on its organizational competency in areas such as business strategy, technology, and exploitation of its technology. While many firms have tremendous competency in business strategy as well as in information technology, they have overlooked the highly important competency of how to utilize technology to serve its strategic goals. The earlier a firm begins to understand how to harness the true value of IS/IT, the better chance it has of enjoying continued success. It is never too early to consider the best way to exploit technology to benefit the business. Through the use of hybrid managers, a small firm may obtain many of the same benefits from exploiting IT as large corporations.

Best Practice Guidelines for Emerging Firms

1) Decide what generic mix of individual skills and defined organizational processes is most appropriate for the firm. Do this by analyzing the firm's mission, the type of industry it is involved in and where it currently resides in its life cycle. Allocate resources accordingly.

2) Do not let the hectic pace or external demands to *Do* lessen your dedication towards *Think*. Investing resources towards *Think* will greatly benefit the firm in the future when funding is no longer scarce.

3) Understand that the firm's culture begins to take shape from day one. Your perseverance towards the role of *Think* will influence organizational norms similarly. Overuse of *Do* will influence the firm to operate in an *ad hoc* way. A certain amount of ad hoc operations must be tolerated but should be monitored.

4) Define and document organizational processes. First target this effort on those processes that will create the largest increase in organizational deftness and significantly decrease the need for highly skilled individuals. Do not forget to re-visit Guideline #1 to maintain a proper balance between defined processes and required individual skills.

5) Categorize all IT projects as Support, Key Operational or Strategic.

6) Attempt to use off-the-shelf solutions for Support Systems, and slightly customized packages for Key Operational Systems. Do <u>not</u> outsource strategic systems.

7) Minimize features of key operational systems. Provide only what is absolutely needed by the firm until proper IT staff can be afforded to create and maintain a more advanced system. This will require effective negotiation between the business division and the technology division of the firm.

8) Allocate a proper level of resources to the role of *Coordinate* according to the type of system (support, key operational or strategic). The role of *Coordinate* is critical for Strategic Systems, somewhat necessary for Key Operational and much less necessary for simple support systems.

9) Utilize Hybrid Managers to perform the role of *Coordinate*. Their role will help align the firm's business and IS/IT strategies where it is most important.

10) Focus 80% the firm's resources and IT efforts on Strategic Systems.

5. IT Implementation[*]

It is estimated that between 50% - 75% of global software maintenance efforts are devoted to legacy systems (DiToro, 2003). Almost all Fortune 1000 organizations rely on legacy systems in order to accomplish day-to-day business processes. Moreover, a recent survey estimates between 11,000 and 13,000 sites in the U.S. are using mainframe computing environments. Many of these legacy systems are considered to be mission critical, and require close to 100% availability in order to ensure business continuity. Unfortunately, by definition legacy systems are outmoded or antiquated, because they either run on outdated platforms or unsupported systems. The system's need for high availability and tight integration between hardware and software make it extremely difficult for upgrades or updates. For many organizations, bringing their legacy system(s) down is simply not an option, as it would impede on business continuity and cost millions of dollars. Boldly stated, "if a business is idle, that business is losing money." However, businesses evolve with

[*] This chapter was prepared by R Hopper, B Migliaccio, M Morgan under the tutelage of Dr. Gurpreet Dhillon, Virginia Commonwealth University.

technology, and business solutions that were implemented five, ten, or even thirty years ago may not be relevant to today's fast-paced, globally integrated world. The question is, at what point do businesses begin modifying or replacing these systems? The caveat is that organizations cannot run the risk of downtime due to systems updates or upgrades, but they also cannot risk downtime and lag time from system obsolescence.

A legacy system, in terms of hardware is generally an older computer running on older components. Mainframes like IBM's System 360 and 390, or a minicomputer like the IBM AS/400, are all examples of legacy systems in terms of hardware. Software can also be classified as legacy. Legacy applications are applications which were written over a long period. Generally these applications are written in antiquated coding languages such as COBOL/CICS, FORTRAN and PL/1, and use outdated data systems like VSAM, IMS/DB and Adabas.

The Giga Information Group estimates that 70 percent or more of the world's active business applications are written in COBOL and 16,000 large enterprises worldwide still use COBOL. The Gartner Group estimates there are 200 billion lines of COBOL code running worldwide. (Seacord et al. 2003, Pg 332).

The Desire for Change

As organizations begin to compete on a global scale, the Web becomes the only viable solution to carry out business processes. The ability to work in remote locations while creating virtual offices remains the number one reason for organizations to utilize Web technologies and Web-enable their legacy systems. Gone are the days when workers were slaves to their desks, or competition was based on geographic location. The widespread use of the Internet and rapid growth in technologies such as XML, CORBA, DCOM, LDAP and other Web Services, has influenced organizations to construct network-centric architectures in order to take advantage of the Web. Companies today rely not only on the Internet for business activity, but also rely on Intranets and Extranets. From accounting to finance to plant and quality management; virtually all facets of business processes have been migrated to some sort of Web architecture. ERP tools such as SAP and PeopleSoft has provided out-of-the-box solutions for organizations to take advantage of Web technologies. Unfortunately, utilizing the Web requires organizations to port and integrate their legacy systems to distribute Web-enabled environments, so that the functionality of the legacy systems can be leveraged without having to rebuild the systems. Web-enabling is not the only reason organizations may decide to upgrade their legacy systems. In a recent white paper by SofwareMining, Dr. Cyrus Montakab states that the biggest reason for organizations to upgrade their legacy systems will be because of B2B integration, coupled with continuous minor changes and requirement alterations. (Dr. Montakab, 2005). As global competition increases, the need for smooth B2B transactions will also increase and will positively correlate to modified GUI and faster response requisitions. An aging legacy system which has begun to deteriorate in quality may create a need for change as well. In a recent study five main symptoms were identified in legacy systems that were aging (Bianchi, Caivano, Marengo, & Visaggio, 2003).

- "pollution, i.e. the system includes many components which do not serve to carry out business functions;

- embedded knowledge, i.e. the knowledge of the application domain and its evolution is spread over the programs and can no longer be derived from the documentation;

- poor lexicon, i.e. the names of components have little lexical meaning or are in any case inconsistent with the meaning of the components they identify;

- coupling, i.e. the programs and their components are linked by an extensive network of data or control flows;

- layered architectures, i.e. the system's architecture consists of several different solutions that can no longer be distinguished; even though the software started out with a high quality basic architecture, the superimposition of these other hacked solutions during maintenance has damaged its quality."

When these systems begin to show signs of aging, the organizations initiate plans for upgrading or modernizing their legacy systems. Therefore, there may not be so much a desire for change in organizations when faced with aging legacy platforms; rather, there is a business need for change. The five above mentioned symptoms of aging legacy systems are proof enough that businesses ignore these issues at their peril. While decision-makers or other stake-holders may have a desire for rapid change to stay abreast of the dynamic world in which they operate, there are challenges. The exigencies of change do not always allow for change to occur over-night. A measured, sober approach to change is appropriate.

The Problem

To create a comparable analogy, a legacy system is like a biological system. The system has many different modules that act like different organs, and the data is the blood stream. It is very difficult to simply replace an organ without ensuring first that the rest of the body won't reject the new module. Moreover, all the modules, or organs, are critical for the whole system to operate correctly. In addition, the blood stream, or data, gets pushed out to other legacy systems among different channels. This brings an extreme level of complexity to the design and to the re-engineered system. The IT team must account for all of its modules and all of external systems which use the system's data. Therefore, it is imperative that the organization utilize the people who know the system inside and out. Herein lays the largest problem and the biggest caveat; the people who know the system the best are generally the people who wrote the system; however, most of these systems were written 10 to 30 years ago, with minor modifications over the years, and the authors of these systems are long gone. Without a thorough knowledge of how the system works and how it interfaces with other outside system, any efforts to rewrite the legacy system will be doomed to failure. Moreover, any system that interfaces with the legacy structure will suffer.

The largest obstacle associated with upgrading an organization's legacy system is re-engineering the systems platform. When an organization is forced to upgrade a legacy system, a complete overhaul of code must be applied; for example, the challenge for software engineers has, in recent years, been to transform and replicate COBOL applications to new languages such as Java or one of Microsoft's .NET languages. In order to complete the task, an overhaul is needed. Java applications that replicate the function of the COBOL applications need to be written in such a way that it is understood by the Java specialist rather than COBOL specialist (Montakab, 2005). Likewise if an organization would like to web-enable their legacy system, the organization will need to completely redesign and overhaul the legacy system's back end. The problem with web-enabling legacy systems is that they are not designed as Web applications. Generally, web applications are loosely coupled, component-based programs, which consist of three tier architecture; user interface, business logic and related databases (Zou & Kontogiannis, 2003). The user interface is accessed through a Web browser while the business logic runs on an application server, communicating though a set of protocols such as XML, HTTP and SOAP. In contrast, legacy systems are generally located on a central location with all the tiers interconnected. A legacy system's architecture may be defined as decomposable, semi decomposable, or non-decomposable (Brodie

& Stonebaker, 1995). Decomposable system architecture means that the three tiers are considered to be distinct components with defined interfaces. This architecture is the best candidate for migration, because the separation of code is similar to that of Web architecture. Alternatively, a semi decomposable system only separates the user interface and the business logic as distinct components, while non-decomposable system architecture has one component that interconnects the three tiers. These systems are more difficult to migrate, because the interaction and separation of the components are more difficult to understand. Non-decomposable are often the most difficult to upgrade, because they are often treated as a sort of 'black box' which functionality and design cannot be alterable (Zou & Kontogiannis, 2003).

Alternatives

Inevitably, as technology prospers, organizations will be faced with the pressures of evolving alongside their more valued business assets. Organizations will be forced to make decisions as to how they will respond to their obsolete and antiquated systems. Essentially, an organization has three alternatives for addressing a legacy system:

- Leave it alone

- Continuous improvement and workarounds

- Re-engineer the system (rip-and-replace).

These three alternatives are all legitimate and appropriate options for organizations to consider when contemplating the fate of a legacy system.

Leave it alone

At times simply leaving a legacy system unchanged is the solution that makes the most sense for organizations. Many reasons could attribute for this option being the optimal solution, lack of financial resources, lack of knowledgeable IT resources, or it is simply not in line with the business strategy. Take Zara for example: Zara is a leading European retailer whose strategic advantage involves efficiently utilizing their in-house distribution and manufacturing channels in order to keep costs low and products revolving. Their niche is providing new products and new lines of clothes every two weeks to their fashion-conscious customers. Zara has the ability to get products from the drawing boards to the stores in as little as 2 weeks, while their competitors take as long as 6 months. The fast rate of production and unique style of distribution enable Zara to respond to the fast-changing and unpredictable tastes of its target customers.

In the summer of 2003, when the technical leads contemplated upgrading the legacy system, Zara's POS system was still running the unsupported DOS operating system on outdated terminals, with antiquated means of communication and data distribution (Mcaffe, Dessain, & Anders, 2006). The initial proposal of upgrading the legacy system was initiated, because the organization was looking for ways to receive up to the minute accurate sales data in order to continually produce relevant product lines which would appeal to demand. However, their ultimate underlying concern was the aging system itself, and lack of vendor support. Zara was faced with the decision of upgrading their system's OS or risk using POS on the old operating system. On the one hand, upgrading would ensure system support and allow the organization to easily integrate new technology to assist production and distribution. On the other hand, the old system had a knowledge base and it worked perfectly. The end result involved Zara's IT department leaving the system untouched. The reasoning behind the decision was that their system worked like clockwork. Sales data was being tracked around the world on a daily basis, and the system experienced little to no problems. The risk involved in upgrading was deemed too risky and too much of a liability, whereas the old system worked, and vendor support wasn't much of an issue when problems didn't arise. At its core, Zara realized that upgrading and modifying their systems was not aligned with their business strategy.

Continuous improvement and workarounds

An organization that needs to integrate with a new technology, perhaps with DMDC or LDAP, may choose not to re-engineer the entire legacy system, but rather apply minor changes in order to incorporate the new technology. This option may be ideal if an organization tries strategically to align their business processes with IT. However, they must remain under budget, or stay within time restrictions. As an example, Washington State University opted to launch an SQL gateway project which allowed them to modernize their systems by enabling new systems written in new languages to issue SQL queries against their legacy database. Essentially, WSU found a way to work around their existing system in order to utilize the data structure without having to rebuild or modify existing legacy code. The advantage to using this approach is that programmers don't necessarily have to know how the whole system works, at best they need to understand how to extract the data they need, and they must understand their project scope. Because of the little integration needed, IT can get the project started and completed relatively quickly. This approach is generally better accepted by the financiers and stakeholders of companies. In the case of Washington State, creating a workaround in lieu of replacement and migration saved the organization an estimated $30 to $50 million dollars (Ruth, 2006).

This legacy issue is not just an American IT issue either. In an article "Australian Orgs Must Keep Legacy Systems" Stan Beer argues that preserving and extending legacy systems is arguably faster, more cost effective and less risky approach that should be considered when weighing the options and issues of upgrading

(Beer, 2005). In his book Data Warehousing, Paul Westerman states that if organizations are going to go with this approach they must take into the account the ease of data transfer and database compatibility so that information can be transferred from older, classical operating systems (Westerman, 2000).

The unfortunate side effect and disadvantage of implementing a workaround is that the legacy system gets more complicated and convoluted. This popular approach to addressing application problems is really considered a hack, or temporary patch to a leaky, ready to explode pipe. As technology continues to evolve, these systems, which utilize many different languages and coding approaches, will make decrypting the algorithms extremely difficult. Eventually the only salvageable asset these systems will procure is the data. The data, however, will be useless unless there is a system in place to utilize it.

Re-engineer the system

Almost no organization has been successful in completely replacing its legacy system, aside from possibly Walmart. Walmart spent billions of dollars in their efforts at re-engineering a system from the ground up. However, this is not a viable solution for most enterprises. It is however, causing pressure among other companies to look at their systems in order to stay competitive in this market. "The bringing of technology into the supermarket industry has probably been forced by Walmart," says John E. Metzger, senior vice president and CIO of A&P a 144 year of company that in 2002 went through a $250 million system and supply chain overhaul. "If we didn't start investing early on, we were dead". There are times when organizations may require re-design or re-engineering of their systems in order for the enterprise to accomplish its goals. But generally when an organization must migrate to a new platform or web-enable and integrate their systems, an organization must undergo an overhaul and re-design in order to rebuild the system. However, because of limited resources, mainly knowledge and cost, organizations instill a rip-and-replace approach. This approach removes modules and updates the code and plugs the new modified code back into the old system. In 2007 a deal was struck with SAP ERP Financials to replace Walmart's legacy system. The plan was to integrate SAP financials with remaining internal systems over a three-year time frame wrapping up in 2010. (Information week, 2007). This rollover is happening in phases as to not lose revenue by the loss of production or freezing of business during changeovers.

Nextel Communications, which provides wireless voice and data services primarily to the business community, provides services to thousands of communities across the United States, including 197 of the top 200 markets, and more than 10 million customers, including 80 percent of the FORTUNE 500 companies (Cap Gemini Ernst & Young, 2004). With the growth of Nextel's customer base, and its challenges with antiquated legacy customer care and billing system, Nextel quickly realized that a world-class customer care and billing system would be critical to their ability in delivering business needs effectively. This decision meant that a conversion of its legacy billing system was essential and thus Nextel chose to complete a business Systems Overhaul project (Cap Gemini Ernst & Young, 2004). Nextel hired Ernst & Young to support multiple system development life cycle functions in order to achieve successful conversion to the new system. The system uses a common database which integrates ten critical business functions.

Seacord, Lewis, and Plakosh cite six possible solutions to the problem of reengineering legacy systems: evolvable software development, software reengineering and modernization, use of commercial components, hardware improvements, web and Internet, and advanced programming languages and tools. (Seacord, et al., 2003 Pg 332).

- Evolvable software development is the construction of systems that are more easily modified through more intelligent systems design factors such modularity with high cohesion and loose coupling. The cost associated with reengineering efforts may cause IT management to invest more resources toward better systems designs.

- Maintenance costs could also drive organizations to invest in software reengineering efforts in hopes of minimizing maintenance costs.

- It is an axiom in systems development that it is easier and cheaper to buy than build. Replacing all or part of a legacy system with commercial, off-the-shelf software components will reduce maintenance effort and costs.

- New hardware and whole new technologies may allow businesses to reevaluate the need for some legacy systems all together. Web publication may soon eliminate the need to many forms of printed material. Legacy printing systems may not need to be reengineered.

- The Internet itself is driving reengineering. As businesses move more and more to an e-commerce model, legacy applications that are unsuitable to an Internet economy will need to be reengineered or replaced to support the new realities.

- New programming languages, tools and techniques off the promise of rapid systems development and the construction of better software in a shorter time. Object oriented programming (OOP), agile development, and graphical software development environments, and advanced testing tools enable software developers to construct systems that are demonstrably correct with greater ease and speed that has ever been possible before.

Another alternative for migrating legacy applications is the use of modeling languages. Unified Modeling Language (UML) is a standardized modeling language used to create abstractions of system components and processes. EGL (Enterprise Generation Language) is an IBM product for describing software systems. Generalized and standardized modeling languages are supported by many software development environments and can aid the reengineering of legacy systems. A drawback to modeling languages is that they are designed to represent object-oriented systems. Most legacy systems are written using procedural coding methods. (Millham, 2005).

Modernization Failures

There have been many examples of legacy system modernization failures and success. The most noteworthy failure adventure was at Ford Motor Company. After five years, 350 IT staffers, and nearly 400 million dollars, Ford was forced to abandon the project and revert to using the old legacy system (Keefe, 2004). At the height of the e-commerce rush, Ford Motor Company decided to replace their collection of 30 aging purchasing and procurement systems, which were aimed at increasing processing speed and cutting cost. The effort to consolidate their systems was intended to serve as a one stop Web-based system that would serve multiple tiers of suppliers, which would initiate large amounts of cost savings into an industry whose margins are already paper thin. Ford's problems started with poor project management, and most specifically poor planning for controlling cost. At its core the project, code name "Everest," suffered from a problem that many legacy modernization projects experience, and that is lack of impact. Ford spent $400 million dollars to migrate its legacy system to the web; so what? The number one rule in process re-engineering is the ability to increase efficiency by a degree of magnitude. Often companies want to be on the leading edge of technology and migrate to the next big thing; however, if the IT endeavor does not align with the business strategy the project will inevitably be a failure. Suppliers were spending long and frustrating hours trying to complete some tasks with the new system, while still reverting to the base system to complete other tasks. The biggest disappointment was that the new system couldn't even do what the old system could. Eventually Ford adopted its fallback option which was to continue using the legacy systems. This however, should raise a red flag for the analyst; if the legacy system is workable, perhaps the company should reassess the initial reasons for launching the project.

Ford is not alone. The Standish Group issued a report in 1995 titled "CHAOS" documenting two software projects that the report categorized as failures. Both projects were canceled before completion. The California DMV driver's license project of 1987 was canceled by 1993 after spending $45 million dollars. The report stated that the "project failed because of internal state politics, unclear objectives, and poor planning." American Airlines had to settle a lawsuit with Budget Rent-A-Car, Marriott Corp. and Hilton Hotels after the failure of its $165 million CONFIRM car rental and hotel reservation system project. (The Standish Group 13 June 2009)

Considerations

When considering the alternatives, organizations must evaluate many variables in order to achieve an optimal solution.

ROI

The most important variable associated with any project of this degree involves completely understanding the cost benefit analysis and ROI. According to a Computerworld periodical published in October 2001, 83% of companies do not track or measure ROI on technology projects, and the reason is because ROI is extremely difficult to measure (Dr. Montakab, 2005). Fear may also play a factor in ROI analysis, as project owners and management my skew the numbers to reflect "successful" project completion. Accountability is critical when calculating ROI and it is thus important not to allow emotion to interfere with data calculations. The numbers generated from ROI analysis should drive the decision as to whether or not IT should undergo such a large and financially crippling project. Obviously if the numbers do not add up in favor of modernization, companies should definitely steer away from legacy modernization. Although this may seem elementary, the fact is many organizations do not understand or incorrectly interpret the ROI numbers. Companies must take a step back and ask themselves does this project make financial sense, and will the final product pay a degree of magnitude more in returns?

In a Computerworld interview, Harwell Thrasher, author of Boiling the IT Frog, stated:

> *"Most people would agree that the right projects are those that are in the best interest of the company and make the most strategic sense. But there are two fallacies in using ROI to choose your projects. First is that the project with the highest ROI is best for the business. That's not necessarily so. For example, a high-ROI project may make a process more efficient by making it more rigid, when what you really need is for it to be more flexible. The second fallacy is that you can compare the ROI of project proposals. Those who write proposals tend to overstate return, understate expenses, minimize transition costs and dependencies on other projects, and neglect risk. So the project with the highest ROI on paper tends to be the one with the most creative proposal writer."* (Melymuka). *He stated that ROI estimates on IT projects are inherently risky propositions.*

Michael Gentile, author of IT Success! Towards a new model for information technology, made a number of statements contradicting traditional IT ROI calculations in a Computerworld interview. He rejected the often-used analogy comparing IT projects to building construction. Gentile stated: "The fundamental error of reasoning in the traditional IT business model is to assume software can be conceived upfront like a house, and subsequently scoped, spec'd and signed off for commitment by both client and vendor -- and that the documented business benefits will start flowing once the solution has been delivered." He further argued that IT projects are fundamentally different from physical construction projects because they are integrated into the whole of the enterprise rather than standalone entities such as buildings.

According to a report released by Nucleus Research Inc., only 37% of companies using service-oriented architecture (SOA) technology report positive return on investment. (Havenstein) The article describes conflict of interest problems in project ROI calculations since the benefits are most directly felt in parts of organizations that do not directly invest resources in the SOA projects. Other conflict of interest issues arise from the fact that many "ROI calculators" are provided by vendors that want to sell more products and services.

Recent discussions of ROI calculations make a distinction between tactical and strategic IT projects. Tactical projects deal with commodity IT products and services where cost savings is the primary factor. Strategic IT products must take into account intangible factors such as customer satisfaction, better user interfaces, or combining databases to facilitate data mining. While the costs of such projects are easy to calculate, the potential benefits are not. This stratification of IT projects allows for intangible benefits to be factored into strategic IT project planning according to Steve Andriole, a professor of business technology at Villanova University. "It has phenomenal implications for project prioritization and ROI. To a great extent, Nick Carr was right -- operational technology has been commoditized." (Anthes).

Project Management

When it comes to transformational projects, the stakes and risks are extremely high; analysts agree that roughly 40% of all IT projects fail. In addition, as the project grows bigger in size and complexity, the rate of success diminishes. Take for example the Hewlett-Packard and Compact merger. Hewlett-Packard successfully consolidated over 70 applications; however, the organization tripped over the deployment of an order processing system which not only messed up orders and angered suppliers, but according to HP the incident crippled their third quarter numbers for 2004 (Keefe 2004).

A large blame for project failures is attributed to poor project management and poor planning. Projects of this magnitude naturally involve too many components and factors. Take for example the biological system metaphor used earlier; the system has many interrelated organs with a colossal blood stream of data. When an organization is about to modernize a legacy system, it is like a group of doctors transplanting multiple organs at once. The risk and preparation for one transplant is daunting enough. Adding another transplant brings the complexity to another level. The doctors must ensure the anesthesia lasts through the whole operation, they must ensure that the correct organs are placed into the patient, and ensure that the hospital is fully staffed so that resources aren't pulled from surgery. Bouncing back to legacy modernization, project management must make certain that every component is well understood, extremely well documented, and that the IT staff knows what is expected at all times.

Nextel could not have accomplished its replacement initiatives without the help of Ernst & Young. The third party consultant group was able to provide enough professional expertise, outside objectivity and leadership that Nextel couldn't have possibly replicated on their own. Analysts accused Ford Motor Company of having weak project managers in charge of such a large endeavor, stating that the project was poorly managed from the beginning, and the initial concept and scope of the project was invalid. It is up to the project managers to fully quantify project specifications, and clearly the folks at Ford missed the target. Many of the employees who tried to use the upgraded system said that the new system completely missed some critical functionality. Planning, another critical element to a project management, encumbers legacy modernization. Planning drives the success of project management; project management is concerned with keeping tasks on time and on budget. Without planning, projects could never remain under budget and on schedule. Legacy system modernization requires extra planning, as they are much larger and often more impactful than any other project an organization can endure, and unfortunately these types of projects are often multi-year assignments. Planning for such a long project creates blurry directions and planners often have too difficult of a time planning so far ahead. The underlying problem for project managers and project management in general, is that we do not know how to manage such large projects. The science behind the 'PMI' is not precise enough, or has not evolved enough for legacy modernization. The tools and techniques used by the certified PMP professionals are not astute enough for this caliber of projects. With that said, some project management is better than none at all. In the case of Nextel, a large specialized firm was able to come in and take control. Many organizations do not relinquish PM control, and that is why Nextel was able to successfully integrate a new system. As more companies begin to embark on larger IT endeavors, the quality and accuracy of project management techniques will improve.

Recognizing that traditional project management puts unrealistic expectations on the project manager, a new approach has been proposed. Grouped under the term "Project Management 2.0", a collection of new tools and techniques has been adopted by a number of organizations, notably Stanford University and Salesforce.com. Project Management 2.0 stresses collaboration and interaction within the project team rather than a hierarchical approach with the project manager directing and controlling all activities. It leverages social networking technologies such as wikis and blogs to facilitate communication and collaboration among the project team members. In his paper Project Management 2.0: The Ultimate Benefits of the New Approach to Project Management presented at the 2nd Annual University of Texas Dallas Project Management Symposium, Andrew Filev described five key benefits of Project Management 2.0: easy collaboration vs. complexity, wisdom of the whole team vs. single mind, many-to-many structure flexibility vs. stiff one-to-many hierarchies, the bigger picture vs. narrow scope view, and productivity boost vs. team's reluctance. He described how hierarchical project management methodologies achieve limited value with an increasing number of participants since the project manager is limited in how many project team members he or she can effectively manage. The value curve achieved by an increasing number of participants flattens as the number of participants reaches the limit of the number of team members the project manager can effectively manage. In contrast, the collaborative nature of project management 2.0 suffers much less from this phenomenon since the team members do not have to interact solely with the project manager to contribute and coordinate efforts. This factor alone shows great promise for legacy reengineering projects, which tend to be large-scale and highly complex requiring many participants.

The Need

Understanding need is a critical component which could save an organization millions of dollars and years of frustration. All too often organizations feel pressure to upgrade technology to avoid obsolescence. To offer a bit of multi-billion dollar consulting advice: "If it ain't broke don't fix it!" Fear of being out-dated or lagging behind competitors fuels managers to stay ahead of the curve, and the desire to be on the cutting edge of technology often drives bad decisions. The Ford disaster is a prime example: instead of focusing on their business niche, Ford pushed forward with the legacy upgrade and lost $400 million dollars and wasted five years. The end result for Ford was relapsing back to their legacy system. The executives should be asking themselves- if the system works, what was the need for modernization? Justifying the modernization effort is an essential task as part of the strategic business plan. If the end result is a quantifiable increase in efficiency and cost savings, modernization plans are easily justified. The obvious mistake of rolling-out a far too-complicated system in too-rapid a time-frame is unjustifiable. To violate this principal, the company would have to envision a leap in strategic capabilities that would justify the potential risk. There are potential benefits that don't fit neatly into an ROI calculation.

The Future

The future for legacy systems is very daunting; as we are living in an interesting and technologically evolving era. "Legacy Modernization" has been a developing progression, which has been historically an incremental improvement process. The first wave of modernization was "screen scraping", which involved transferring monochromatic command line interfaces to newer and exciting graphical user interfaces. Eventually continuous improvement brought the legacy systems to the Web world (New Legacy Modernization Strategies and Disciplines). Unfortunately all the continuous improvements have created a complicated mess which will become unsalvageable. Organizations have components that are unmanageable, simply because nobody in the agency can understand how it works; too many pipelines connecting to each module make the legacy system extremely convoluted and interconnected. As technology becomes more advanced, integration will become next to impossible, whether it's because of the gap in technologies, or because the interwoven pipelines connect to too many other outside systems. Because there is a web of interconnected legacy systems that communicate across many different organizations, all organizations will have to all agree to upgrade. Frighteningly enough, the trend moving forward will be to replace the legacy system completely, and many organizations will fail, while some will drive their businesses into the ground trying to accomplish this impossible task. The reason for this cataclysmic event is because of new market penetration. As new companies enter the market, older companies will have to remain competitive and respond to technological changes which may change market strategy. There will always be new companies entering the market, and they have the newer technology that can threaten the older players. Best Buy for example is infinitely more successfully than Circuit City and it is no secret that Circuit City has been struggling for many years trying to modernize their systems. Sadly, as soon as a new company opens its doors, it already has a one up advantage over its seasoned competitors, and that is lack of baggage.

Ironically Circuit City was considered an industry leader as recently as 2001. In his best selling business book, Good to Great, author Jim Collins cited Circuit City over rivals Silo, Tandy, and Best Buy as one of the companies that demonstrated marked performance gains compared to its competitors. One of the reasons for Circuit City's past excellence was its use of technology accelerators. In his chapter on technology accelerators, Collins noted that Circuit City:

Pioneered application of sophisticated point-of-sale and inventory-tracking technologies – linked to the concept of being the "McDonald's" of big-ticket retailing, able to operate a geographically dispersed system with great consistency. (Collins, 2001, Pg 300).

It could be argued that the advanced technological platforms that Circuit City built in the past, including its point-of-sale and inventory software systems, became a legacy drain that anchored its strategic systems architecture in the past and prevented it from fully embracing the new technologies of the e-commerce era.

Conclusion

The epic struggles of modernizing legacy systems will progress into the next era of business globalize. As organizations attempt to web enable their systems, more breakthroughs will inevitably unfold. Project management practices and IT planning will be forced to become increasingly more accurate and prevalent. The underlining nature of new competition and technological obsolescence will drive organizations to update their systems; however, the companies that align their business processes with IT infrastructure are the organizations what will survive. It will be the organizations that ask the questions "What do we really need?" and "Can we already accomplish this?" who will succeed in their IT endeavors. The poor planners and big spenders will be left behind with empty pockets and ill-equipped resources.

Information technology is still a very young discipline that has been evolving over the last 50 years. It is a work in progress as new technologies and better processes emerge. Some of this technological change can be predicted and some cannot. Research shows that the first round of companies maxed-out their ability to succeed with the initial technology. These companies rose to the top in terms of success and efficiency when compared to their competitors. However, when the next shift in technology occurred, it made existing systems inefficient or obsolete, leaving those companies at a competitive disadvantage with emerging businesses who were utilizing the newer technology. Currently, Object Oriented Programming is popular. However, it may only last 10-15 years, or only as long as this wave of technology is being ridden. It is difficult to say or predict what the future may hold in terms of IT effectiveness. What is good today may not be good tomorrow. Information technology strategic planning is a truly challenging concept.

Yet there is hope. Recognizing that the status quo is unacceptable, a multi-front war on IT project failure is being waged. Forward-thinking IT organizations are taking an honest look at IT project performance and are attempting to address the failure rate with new research-based methodologies. New practices are emerging that offer the promise of reproducible project management success. Computer science departments at major universities are producing graduates trained to attack programming tasks using commonly accepted techniques that produce code that is rigorous and flexible. New tools for application modeling are emerging along with new products that support them. Collaborative development practices offer the promise of harnessing previously untapped resources for project management, business process re-engineering, and application design. Will these new tools and techniques succeed in consistently delivering projects that are on-time, within budget, and do what they were supposed to do? Or will IT professional still be looking for solutions to replace legacy systems ten years from now? The next decade should prove very interesting.

The decision to upgrade legacy systems is extremely complex. It can be reasonably argued that infrastructure projects and other tactical IT initiatives solved by commodity technology solutions should only be undertaken to achieve clear business benefits yielding quantifiable return on investment. ROI estimates for strategic legacy systems replacement projects are much harder to predict. The organization must also weigh intangible benefits and new capabilities for which ROI is much less certain. In such cases, there is high risk, and these initiatives should only be undertaken when there is the potential for equally high reward.

6. IT and Managerial Discretion*

Managerial discretion can be conceptualized as the range of options a manager is free to pursue in order to pursue long-term strategic performance. Supply chain management, along with other initiatives such as knowledge management, technological innovation and collaborative competition, suggest that efficiency gains accompany collaborative information sharing with suppliers, customers, and even competitors. Other than the presumed competitive intelligence risks associated with sharing proprietary intelligence, the literature has not addressed how the short term operational performance imperatives of collaborative information sharing may create a level of information transparency that can hamper managerial discretion, and thus strategic performance over the long run. We investigate this gap in the literature and provide a conceptual model that provides an insight into managerial discretion and its affect on operational and strategic performance of firms.

* A version of this paper also appears as Fabian, F.H. and Dhillon, G. 2007. Losing Managerial Discretion: The Unexplored Risk of Collaborative Information Sharing. Journal of Information Science and Technology, 4 (1): 50-62. Used with permission.

Introduction

The ability for computerized information systems to enable an increasingly interconnected information network has encouraged research on how information sharing between organizations can increase variables such as productivity, trust, and learning (Arino, de la Torre, & Ring, 2001; Barua, Konana, Whinston & Yin,2004; Greis & Kasarda,1997; Hamel, 1991; Mowery, Oxley, and Silverman, 1996). Perspectives such as supply chain management, knowledge management, technological innovation, and collaborative competition have led firms to offer increasing access to their computer information systems as they pursue information sharing with suppliers, customers, and even competitors (Magretta,1998; Meyer, 1998). Automatic replenishment programs (ARPs) such as Continuous Replenishment Planning (CRP), and Vendor-Managed Inventory (VMI) reflect partnership initiatives based on information sharing among the members in attempts to improve efficiency across the supply chain (Daugherty, Myers, and Autry 1999; Sabath, Autry, and Daugherty 2001). Susarla et al (2004) argue that advances in information technology (IT) that improve coordinated information exchange between firms result in a significant impact on measures of operational efficiency such as time to market, inventory turnover, and order delivery cycle time.

Information sharing between collaborating entities in general raises a number of issues regarding for example confidentiality (Lee and Whang 1998), trust (Simchi-Levi, Kaminsky, and Simchi-Levi 2000; Waller, Johnson, and Davis 1999), technology investments and expenses (Waller, Johnson, and Davis 1999), inventory ownership (Simchi-Levi, Kaminsky, and Simchi-Levi 2000), etc. The literature in the area of federated databases, data warehousing, ontologies and Knowledge Sharing, Semantic Web in the context of information systems (Kishore et al. 2004, Lee et al, 2005, Olsen et al. 1994, Sharman et. al, 2004) deal with technical issues of sharing information. Though issue of information sharing has been studied from a more technical perspective and from the perspective of improving supply chain efficiency have been well studied and there is a vast extant of literature in this area, there are many aspects that remain inadequately addressed.

However from a content perspective the area information sharing has been understudied. The literature in regard to the appropriate level of collaborative information sharing, has been overwhelmingly framed along efficiency criteria and its benefits (Gordon and Leob, 2003; Gal-Or and Ghose, 2005). This chapter investigates the issue of the loss of managerial discretion on account of information sharing and its impact on the long term strategic competitiveness of firms. For the purpose of bringing better clarity to the discussion we conceptualize 'Managerial discretion' in the context of information sharing as the discretionary authority available to the manager as a consequence of the asymmetry of information. Thus managerial discretion reflects the range of options a manager is free to pursue in order to garner long-term strategic performance. For example like a card game, if a partner firm can "see all of the cards" in another firm's hand, many strategic and tactical options will be closed off for that exposed firm, -- for example, if prices must reflect greater access to information (Bester & Ritzberger, 2001).

Here, we are interested in elaborating information security concerns from allowed access in collaborative information sharing that may lead to the potential for harming long-term strategic performance. In particular, we examine how transparency has the potential for constraining a manager's discretion, i.e. the range of strategic options the manager can pursue. The current literature mostly focuses on operational performance however we contend that the loss of managerial discretion leads to loss of strategic options.

The contributions of this paper are two-fold. First it provides a theoretical framework for the notion of loss of managerial discretion. Second the paper develops a conceptual model that provides an insight into managerial discretion and its affect on operational and strategic performance of firms.

Related Background

Below we define the construct of managerial discretion and provide a model for thinking about how to assess whether collaborative information sharing arrangements threaten its optimal use. In particular, we set an agenda for investigating this phenomenon further by positing a role for trust and absorptive capacity in mediating the effect of transparency on discretion.

What is Collaborative Information Sharing?

Joint ventures and strategic alliances have burgeoned as "hybrid" organizations with distinct competitive advantages (Doz & Hamel, 1998). These relationships, that often stress horizontal linkages between firms, are theoretically able to provide "relational rents" (Dyer & Singh, 1998) such as increased rents through joint production, or the opportunity to learn from each other (Hamel, 1991). Additional prominent goals of alliances and joint ventures are as an entry mode for economies entering modern market competition (Zahra, Ireland, & Hitt, 2000) or to enable innovation and product development (Kotabe & Swan, 1995). Due to the speed of environmental change from globalization and technological progress, it is increasingly difficult for a single firm to possess the resources needed to develop and sustain both current and future competitive advantages (Harrison, Hitt, Hoskisson & Ireland, 2001). Successful collaborative information sharing is key where in some industries over half, of research, value chain, sales and marketing alliances are arranged as "virtual alliances," with staffs that are not co-located and no physical alliance entity exists (Rule, Ross & Donougher,1999).

Additionally, the interlocking of firms in supply chain relationships has also implied vast changes in information sharing and thus firm interactions (Greis & Kasarda,1997; Hart & Saunders, 1995). These relationships are often spurred by the substantial efficiencies in logistics and development that collaborative information sharing can extract (Cachon & Fisher, 2000), leading to impressive progress in supply chain management and customer relationship management platforms. Indeed these technological capabilities may spawn increased collaboration: for instance, ocean freight terminal owners are pressured to provide additional services (such as monitoring manufacturer's rail cars, tank trucks, and barges) due to the capabilities in new terminal information technologies (Westervelt, 2002).

These interfirm relationships, therefore, are commonly bolstered by new abilities for collaborative information sharing between the firms. Ten or more years ago this sharing represented only the minimum of capabilities based on email, ftp systems, and limited "log on" capabilities to databases via land lines. Electronic information transfer was but a speedier option than "snail" mail. In contrast, systems evolving over the last decade allow outsiders access to their needed data, but often such access is integrated with a larger set of electronic corporate data (Upton & McAfee, 1996). Firm policies that monitor access space or usage have generally not evolved accordingly, and the strategic ramifications of such transparency for discretion has been unexamined. An example illustrates the vast difference in allowing access to a firm's information base through current electronic means versus physical interactions.

Access controls provide only the needed access to entities. But determining the access needs based on operational needs defines the relationship between firms. This information sharing is referred to as collaborative information sharing. In this paper we examine information sharing in collaborative environments from the perspective of loss of managerial discretion.

Below we review the progress of theory about collaborative information sharing, and the accompanying theoretical emphasis, from the strategic point of view. In much of the above description of the phenomenon, a major driver of collaborative information sharing has been its ability to improve operational performance via adopted efficiencies. Yet, the evolution of the phenomenon also necessitates changing stances on the impact of these interactions for strategic management, and we believe that recognition of the implications for managerial discretion is warranted. This current reconsideration of the benefits of information sharing, then, reflects the advances in interlocking information systems in the last five years that have radically

Theoretical Foundations

Strategic management research has borrowed heavily from economics. Inter-firm research therefore historically focused on the intensity of rivalry between firms (Oster, 1990; Porter, 1985) and thus did not address collaborative information sharing. Indeed, collaboration between competitors, in particular, was viewed as an attempt at collusion (Genesove & Mullin, 2001; Stiglitz, 1968), and any other information "sharing" fell under the category of espionage. Thus, under this paradigm of competition, aggressive competitive intelligence and defensive security of proprietary information were critical.

Given this early legacy, it is not surprising that little research directly differentiates the strategic need to restrict collaborative information sharing from that of guarding against hostile access. Therefore, the loss of important proprietary information has generally been the key consideration in regard to models positing theoretical criteria for information restrictions; e.g., the consideration of sharing criteria for foreign direct investment decisions (Hennart, 1982).

Indeed, competitive intelligence research seldom extends beyond the issue of blocking information leaks to unintended parties, rather than designing effective information sharing strategies in collaborative environments. For instance, Helms et al (2000) do prescribe prioritizing information for sharing, but do not provide theoretical criteria for assessing threats to strategic options. Kanter and Myers (1991) point out that collaboration may change a focal firm in unforeseen ways - by altering power relationships, firm structures, skills and behaviors. Yet beyond these preliminary acknowledgements, by and large, attention has centered on the potential havoc of hostile access to corporate information for competitive intelligence gathering i.e., the need to conduct defense against "information operations" by adversaries in an "information war" (McCrohan, 1998).

Strategic management research, though, has markedly evolved toward a paradigm emphasizing interdependent and cooperative action between firms, rather than stressing a market or hierarchy split (Harrigan, 1988; Powell, 1990; Williamson, 1991). Inter-firm research on collaborative goals like product development (Eisenhardt and Tabrizi, 1995) or on relationship types, such as between customers, (Magrath & Hardy, 1994), research communities or partners; between competitors (Brandenburger & Nalebuff, 1996; Browning, Beyer and Shetler, 1995) and between principals and suppliers (Gold, 1987) has burgeoned. Conceptually, collaboration allows firms to produce more efficiently and effectively by delegating tasks to the firm with the greatest task competence, for instance by a) investing in interfirm specialization (Dyer, 1996); b) employing integrated problem solving (Clark & Fujimoto, 1991; Takeishi, 2001); and c) combining assets for scale and scope economies (Axelrod, 1984). There is also considerable interest in how firms can learn from each other to build dynamic capabilities (Eisenhardt & Martin, 2000). In summation, literature in the last decade has decidedly emphasized the importance of improving the level of information sharing.

Similarly, a rethinking of inter-firm information sharing has accompanied the increase in elaborate forms of alliance. Both the legal community (Cullen, 2000) and competitive intelligence researchers have receptively reconsidered the legalities and advantages of voluntary information sharing (Radcliffe, 2002). In response to this phenomenon, interest began to arise in the great difficulties and expense of trying to share complex assets such as knowledge (Teece, 1977) successfully, i.e. how to make collaborative information sharing more effective. Thus, while some collaboration-related literature has identified hazards to working with potential competitors (Hamel, Doz and Prahalad, 1989), the greater emphasis has been on the difficulty of achieving success. Specifically, incorporating new, externally-derived information for learning and knowledge in a firm is extremely difficult. The absorptive capacity perspective (Levinthal & Cohen, 1991) has provided theoretical antecedents needed for a firm to identify, comprehend and exploit external information. Hart & Saunders (1997) emphasized the importance of trust in motivating specific forms of sharing. Much research has developed variables associated with information transfer for collaborative learning, especially in the international joint venture context (Inkpen, 1997; Lane, Salk, & Lyles, 2001, Lyles & Salk, 1996). In sum, information sharing risks are little emphasized; rather, getting firms to become more transparent and share data is viewed as the overriding concern.

Managerial Discretion. The term managerial discretion has a legacy in the strategy and organizational behavior literature in reference to the "latitude of action" a manager has in pursuing objectives (Hambrick & Finkelstein, 1987). Forces from the environment, the organization, and personal characteristics can constrain the options available to a manager. For instance, a utility and a privately-held computer firm face very different options in regard to pricing and service options based on environmental constraints (Finkelstein & Hambrick, 1990). In general, an important implication of the managerial discretion literature is its ability to bridge the problem of whether managers or environments are more explanatory of firm performance, and in particular, when managers can expect to have greater discretion to indeed affect performance. Other related literature has also revolved around understanding when managers have strategic choice (Child, 1982) and how factors such as politics, action determinism, uncertainty, and the environment can all work to limit the range of options facing a manager (Child, 1997). A central assertion of this literature, though, is that the level of constraints managers face is a boundary on their ability to affect firm performance (Finkelstein & Hambrick, 1987).

For our propositions here it is important to note that Child (1997) recognized a unique connection between access to timely, analyzable, and affordable information and strategic choice. In particular, he drew upon March and Olsen (1976) to note the ability for ambiguity to constrain strategic choice, and concluded that "The degree of choice will therefore be inhibited by limited and or ambiguous information." (1995:52). While this has generally been considered in the case of the manager seeking information to make a discretionary choice, we argue that it also has implications for a manager giving information. In particular, sharing information with another firm can provide greater latitude of action to another manager vis-à-vis to interactions with a focal firm.

Actually, there are indications that managers in the realm of inter-firm alliances and information sharing are already aware that transparency causes some level of constraint in their behavior. Even some of the earliest work immediately acknowledged there could arise difficulties in differentiating organizational boundaries (Estrin, 1987). Hamel, Doz and Prahalad (1989) offers one of the few examples of prescriptions for limiting information sharing based on losing future competitive advantage from competitors' learning. Their research offers some premonition of how a firm's discretion may be harmed by such sharing:

> *"Collaboration doesn't always provide an opportunity to fully internalize a partner's skills. Yet just acquiring new and more precise benchmarks of a partner's performance can be of great value."* (1989:139).

Similarly, Hart & Saunders (1997) provided a framework for thinking about power and trust issues for adopting electronic data interchange (EDI) systems in buyer-seller dyads. They argued that power dependency between firms can cause greater vulnerability under information sharing. In conclusion they advanced that openness, caring and reliability were features that could build trust and address power differences between firms. Yet, their discussion was limited to a more impersonal firm-level of analysis, and the transactive issue of the transfer of standardized documents between buyer and seller. The overwhelming advantages of EDI in their context lend them to state, "Computer networks change the nature of organizational boundaries. They introduce different and potentially more effective methods of coordination between firms; and, their implementation implies that protectionist bargaining strategies must give way to more cooperative relationships with trading partners." (1997;24). It is the latter contention that we share reservations about here. The EDI adoption issues discussed in their article is now no more contentious than the adoption of instant credit card verification. We wonder though, whether there might be some theoretical limit to which collaborative information sharing with other firms can emasculate the bargaining strategies that protect strategic advantage.

A model of Transparency

While both theoretical and empirical discussions indicate the transparency from collaborative information sharing may interfere with managerial discretion, there has been little development of what steps are involved which may harm ultimate strategic performance. We offer two mechanisms by which too much transparency may impact discretion: through increased hyperscrutiny, in which observers begin to demand certain behaviors, and through bargaining exposure, which forecloses specific options a manager might undertake. In both cases a manager's discretion is diminished and potentially, lower strategic performance will entail. Our model is shown in Figure 6.1, and discussed further below.

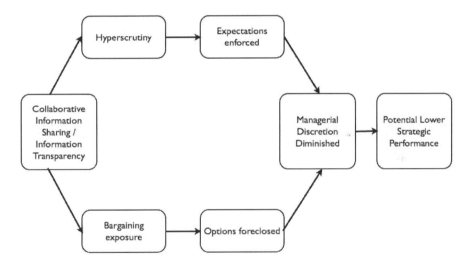

Figure 6.1, A conceptual model of transparency and loss of managerial discretion

Hyperscrutiny refers to when observers are capable of monitoring various facts of another's behavior through information technologies, and then use this information to make decisions which may be premature or oversimplified due to the

145

incompleteness of the monitoring mechanism (Ogilvie & Fabian, 1999). In networked relationships among organizations, the access to (by definition) partial, real-time data offers an audience of a wide set of people who may question when information patterns diverge from their expectations. Specifically, as information and rules become more transparent to others, the ability for a decision maker to use judgment and discretion diminish accordingly (Glazer, Steckels and Winer, 1997).

For instance, a customer in the habit of buying inventory lots on an ad hoc basis may think nothing of the fact that the ability to immediately fill orders is irregular. But, if that customer's interlock with the suppliers database indicates that the firm habitually allotted inventories according to a first come, first-serve basis, and now decides to use a piecemeal allotment across all customers, they may object to such changes and harm the contract's potential, or even threaten litigation.

For managers themselves, the knowledge that their collaboration partners are aware of particular information on an ongoing basis can lead to psychological pressure that encourages suboptimal behaviors. Extreme accountability to unseen audiences for making shared information logical and in accord with expectations, may force managers to adhere to suboptimal regulations over their discretion, hiding discrepant information, or delaying action or information dissemination for superiors to manage (Roberts, Stout & Halpern, 1994). Additionally, decision makers may focus on appearances (Sutton & Galunic,1996) that may ultimately harm innovation and learning (e.g., see Geen, 1991).

Not only does information transparency tend to enforce expectations of continuing consistent behavior, but the movement toward information sharing may also open up vagaries or idiosyncracies of a firm's business practice that a manager may be unwilling or uninterested in sharing. Certainly the standardization of interfaces requires managers to undergo some changes in practice to come into accord with technological specifications; but the revelation of practices is also likely to incur an increase in behavioral expectations, by a collaboration partner. Indeed, transparency is considered a part of the path to trust, but ironically enough, this path may lead to increasing demands for greater trust - through greater transparency (Hart & Saunders, 1997).

In conclusion, a manager under highly collaborative information sharing may find his range of alternatives moved from output satisfaction toward procedural compliance. Such a change is more or less welcome depending upon the demands of the job. For instance, the difference is akin to that of a professor who is required to publish journal articles and meet minimal office hour requirements versus an administrator that must hold regular daily office hours; different jobs suggest different constraints, but some work demands more flexibility especially in cases of a need for creativity (Amabile, 1983).

Bargaining Exposure. Like a card game, if a partner firm can "see all of the cards" in another firm's hand, many strategic and tactical options will be closed off for that exposed firm, for example if prices must reflect greater access to information (Bester & Ritzberger, 2001). Indeed, the role of asymmetries of information in negotiating position is a central premise in much of negotiations theory. The ensuing lack of discretion for decision making may negatively impact performance outcomes (Rajagopalan, 1997).

In an extension of our example above, a customer may be transacting with a supplier in regard to a need to buy from their inventory. If another customer has foreseeable one-time demands or needs, or perhaps is of some special interest to the focal firm in regards to creating a new contract relationship, the focal firm may be interested in reserving a part of the inventory. Yet, if there is transparency on inventory lots, this may constrain the manager's ability to make special accommodations, without "lying" to their database system, which is likely to cause other administrative havoc.

Not surprisingly, information technology, with its ability to increase transparency, has revolutionized the job and responsibilities of managers. Bovens and Zouridis (2002) discuss this phenomenon in the public sector, noting that decision making has moved from the arbitration of individual cases to the design of the overall system. If indeed the increase in transparency across the system results in less ability to provide either special favors to, or hold back favors from, other members in the supply chain on a case by case basis, then the power dependency literature, which examines forms of exchange (Emerson, 1981), can provide some guidance on the implications. Transparency may well change the transaction environment away from a potential "reciprocal environment," in which actors can contribute unilateral favors without any knowledge of potential reciprocation, toward a more negotiated or fixed price environment, (in which all exchanges are bilaterally negotiated). Specifically, because collaborative information sharing may make apparent special treatment to various partners, it may forestall such favor granting to avoid repercussions.

Paradoxically, Molm and colleagues (2003) have found that partners perceive of interactions as less fair the more they interact in a negotiated versus a reciprocal environment. They also note that partners are likely to engage less in transaction environments they perceive to be unfair. Thus, granting too much information transparency may lead to a deterioration of some partner relationships. Interestingly, the crisis management literature emphasizes that the inability to shape what other stakeholders perceive is generally problematic for an organization (Pearson & Clair, 1998). Their general guidelines on handling crises reflect the problems of information transparency in these extreme conditions: there is a need to control access to information -- not necessarily to hide important information, but rather to assure information is not mishandled by uncontained disclosure (Coombs, 1995).

Conclusions

Without a doubt information sharing arrangements among firms have increased the efficiency and productivity of the world economy. Moreover, an increasing number of transactions are amenable to simple digitization which any resistance to would signal economic ignorance. Yet, we believe it is important that strategic imperatives should drive information sharing, rather than technological capabilities.

In this chapter we presented a model of transparency as a constraint on managerial discretion and its theoretical foundations. This model has some limitations in that it does not include factors such as the consequence of exposure to parties that are not able to exploit available information in a timely fashion to prosper on other related projects. Future work includes the development of an empirical study to validate the model. An impact of this study leads to better understanding of information sharing contexts from a more strategic perspective. A more practical application of the model is the development of a second generation of supply chain information sharing architecture where the quantity of information that is shared can be adjusted based on the firm viewing the information across inter-organizational boundaries. This is much needed so as to provide some ability on the part of managers to control the levels of visibility.

7. IS Innovation

In this chapter we discuss how technological innovations come into being and get sustained over a period of time. We present a framework that conceptualizes the nature and scope of *incremental* and *pioneering* innovations. Our characterization of innovation progression within a market setting, helps in identifying and defining mechanisms for establishing leadership strategies, that guide an organization to successfully incorporate a given innovation within their targeted market group.

It is interesting to note that many of the innovations in products and services never see the light of the day. Literature characterizes such failures as 'ahead of its time' (Ali 1996), 'technologically complex (Ning and Xiwen 2007), 'difficult to use' (Tuomi 2000), limited practical benefits' (Tushman and O'Reilly III 2002). Being able to successfully capitalize on identified opportunities or avoid failure of planed innovative opportunities is a function of the leadership. In terms of identifying opportunities a competent leader must be able to visualize potential synergies, which could be created from the dynamic combination of business process and unique resources. Innovative technologies provide an enhancement opportunity for a resource's value and occur when a resource produces greater returns in the presence of the technology than it does alone. Ulrich & Lake (1990) illustrated the strategic importance of identify, managing and leveraging core competencies and their link to sustainable competitive advantage. Technology leadership needs to encompass the skills, which support the identification and exploitation of these innovative opportunities.

This chapter classifies innovations along two dimensions – *incremental* and *pioneering*. *Incremental* innovations are those where there is a marginal improvement in a product or a service. Typically such improvements may result from ensuring efficiency of a business process and implementing limited technology improvements. A key characteristic of an incremental innovation is that any improvement made is intricately linked with the values, aspirations and expectations of the users. Thus when a financial institution provides value added services on top of their existing products (e.g. ability to recharge prepaid mobile phones via a debit card), it is an incremental innovation. It is so, because the customer value proposition does not change remarkably. Prepaid mobile phone users have to recharge their phones and majority of the users do possess an ATM card, so it makes sense to provide such an additional service.

On the other hand, *pioneering* innovations are those, which change the value proposition of the users. Such innovations typically occur through the use of new delivery channels and/or establishing radically new ways of configuring products or services. For instance, when Amazon.com decided to sell books online, the company created a new value proposition. Not only did Amazon.com utilize a new delivery mechanism (i.e. use of the Internet), it also essentially created a new innovative product (the e-book). Today the maker is getting transformed once again with the launch of Kindle and digitization of books, magazines and newspapers. This type of an innovation can be characterized as pioneering because besides introducing a different value proposition to the users and customers, Amazon.com is able to radically redefine the marketplace for books.Various leadership skills for development and exploitation of opportunities are central to ensuring success, whether these may be for incremental or pioneering innovations. What are the characteristics of leadership for each kind of innovation is the theme of this paper. First we discuss the two dimensions that come together to define the nature and scope of incremental and pioneering innovations. Next we characterize as to when an incremental innovation has the potential of becoming a pioneering innovation. We present examples of contexts when a new innovation can establish itself in a given market. Finally, we present a few leadership skills which are helpful to identifying opportunities for utilizing innovative technologies.

Delivery of products and services

In research and practitioner literature delivery of products and services has been classified into three broad delivery channels or classes – delivery via agents; delivery via integrated front-back end supply chains; delivery via network of producers and suppliers in a market (Ciborra 1994). Correspondingly IT systems that support agencies are referred to as agency support systems (e.g. IT systems supporting insurance and travel agents), IT systems supporting integrated supply chains take the form of integrated systems (e.g. clinical information systems in hospital or a typical ERP system in an organization), and IT systems supporting a market network of producers and suppliers is referred to as a market network system (e.g., auction websites such as eBay or shopping networks such as shopping.com).

Agency Support Systems. As the name suggests, an agency is an organization with a particular purpose and largely involves organizing transactions between two parties. IT systems that ensure smooth running and efficiency of such transactions are referred to as agency support systems. Such systems are perhaps the most basic of the three classes of systems in delivering products and services. Agency support systems may be networked within a particular organization locally or may have external links with agency headquarters with which regular synchronizations and update may take place. The purpose of such systems typically is to ensure efficiency in an organization's operations. In the 1980s, agency support systems had been touted to be rather strategic to a business operation largely because the applications provided some advantage in a market place (Galliers 1987). Leaders who had the visionary acumen to identify opportunities for the development and implementation of such systems ensured significant revenue streams to their respective corporations (Earl 1990). In the current environment however agency support systems ensure the basic survivability of a given business. If an agency support system does not exist or is problematic for an organization, then the legitimacy of that organization comes into question for external stakeholders. While agency support systems provided immense competitive advantage at one time, today they are simply essentials to running a business.

Integrated Systems. The word integrated is derived from the Latin word integrat, which means made whole from the verb integrave. When an IT system helps in linking and coordinating various parts of an organization (or other IT systems), then such systems are referred to as Integrated Systems. If agency support systems are holistically linked with front and back end systems, then it emerges to be an integrated system. When order processing for a retailer is intricately linked with order fulfillment, which in turn has an integrated interface with product supplier systems, it is an example of an integrated system. Clinical information systems, electronic medical record systems, materials requirement planning systems and the new generation of Enterprise Resource Planning systems, are all examples of integrated systems.While many companies during the mid

90's sought first mover advantage with the development of one kind of an integrated system or the other, today such systems simply give parity. Integration across functions and business processes, requires good leadership shills, which are essential for success of integrated systems (e.g. see (Nah, Lau et al. 2001), (Wagner and Scott 2003). The advent of integrated systems also ushered in the era of business process re-engineering, which saw radical changes taking place within organizations (e.g. see (Hammer 1990). Since many businesses have jumped onto the re-engineering bandwagon, time use of integrated systems within an organization simply became an issue of necessity, at least for majority of the enterprises.

Market Network Systems. Market networks have always existed. From a network of buyers and sellers from the days of 18th century cotton trade between America and England to the modern day linkages in the Dutch Flower Auctions. While coordination between buyers and sellers was rather straight forward in the case of the cotton trade, linking buyers and suppliers in the Dutch Flower Auctions is a little more complex. Nevertheless market networks do exist and systems that support such markets are the market network systems (Ciborra 1994). The use of market networks systems can be innovative to an industry or just an *organization* depending on the situation. When an organization's leaders identify an opportunity to offer new creative products or services through the use of pioneering technologies, which challenges the status quo via a market network system it is considered to be a pioneering innovation.

While all types of organizational contexts are not relevant in terms of creating a market network system, in situations where it is indeed possible to do so, market network systems can give significant strategic advantage (Ciborra 1993). Such advantages may be in terms of sourcing suppliers and/or buyers, price negotiation or even the opportunity to create new markets. Good examples of market network systems are eBay, Yahoo shopping and the like. Development of any market network system requires corresponding changes in organizational structures as well, which also are typically in the form of networks. In fact over the past several years we have seen a move away from bureaucratic structures to loosely coupled networks (see (Orton and Weick 1990), (Orton and Dhillon 2006). Loosely coupled networks allow for flexibility and agility within an organization. Thereby allowing for innovative leaders to respond to market opportunities in a quick and efficient manner allowing the them an ability to utilize pioneering technologies to achieve a competitive advantage.

Service Type

In the services management literature, different types of services have been classified into three categories – customized services, representing situations where a personalized service may be necessary (e.g. salon or a spa); universal services, where a uniform standardized service is offered (e.g. hospitals, schools); mass transaction, where there is a volume of simple transactions for large number of people (e.g. selling grocery items to customers or other teller banking services).

Customized Services. There are certain classes of products or services, which demand a customized service. While it is important for a Salon or a Spa to offer a customized service, that may not be the case for a large hotel chain. However, a hotel company may aspire to differentiate its services provided to its customers from the mass services provided at the other hotel chains. When the four seasons designed their customer relationship module (CRM) they did just this. They linked their CRM module to the main reservation system so when a customer makes a special request such as extra towels or feather pillows then every future reservation will prompt the question if the customer would like that special request for the new reservation. This type allow four seasons to classify its services as high end customized service, it no longer remains in mass services category. In this case the value proposition gets changed, an issue we shall discuss later in the paper.

Universal Services. These are services, which are pretty standard across the board. Irrespective of who the customer is, they are likely to receive the same kind of service (although many institutions attempt to differentiate themselves along certain dimensions). If one were to visit an urgent care facility in a hospital, the nature, scope and kind of service one receives is pretty much same across the board. Similarly if one were to be enrolled in a state university, the kind of education imparted to the students would be the same across the board. University X may however differentiate itself from University Y on certain grounds – profile of students attracted; funding opportunities; qualification of faculty; average size of classes; etc.

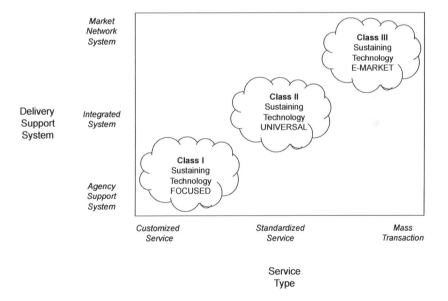

Figure 7.1, Service-Delivery Matrix

Mass Transactions. In the early stages of automation, the emphasis was largely mass transaction. The notion of mass transaction is very similar to that of mass production. Building off a standardized service, mass transactions allow for a large number of straightforward transactions. The focus of mass transactions is efficiency and volume to achieve economies of scale.

A combination of delivery support system type and service type presents three classes of opportunities. We term these Class I, Class II and Class III innovations. While we argue that any improvement within each class is an *incremental* innovation, moving between classes is facilitated by a *pioneering* innovation. There are clearly inefficiency zones when delivery support system type is combined with the service type.

In cases where an *agency support system* is imposed on to support *mass transactions,* the result is rather disastrous and may lead to an unsatisfied group of customers. In the early 1990s a lot of insurance companies automated the collection of personal demographic details and the subsequent sale of insurance policies. While in theory it may be possible to do so, the business model was flawed to begin with. This is because when an *agency support system* gets used to handle mass transactions, errors creep in. Eventually the insurance companies divided the process into two parts – collection of demographic information; sale of a policy. Similarly it does not make sense to use a *market network system* to provide a customized service.

Spotting an Innovation

Given the aforementioned, technological innovations occur within and between classes. When an innovation takes place within a given class, its nature and scope does not necessarily change the value proposition. Hence being incremental, simply extends the life cycle of a given technology. Typically this occurs via enhancements and by ensuring efficiency gains. Innovations of this kind progress along an S-curve. The notion of an S curve was first introduced by Foster (1986) where the performance of a technology is mapped against the effort applied. The core argument of a technology S-curve is that while technology performance increases correspondingly with the degree of effort, it eventually reaches an upper limit or a plateau. At this point improvement would either be impossible or prohibitively expensive. If one were to seek further improvement, a discontinuity is needed in order to switch to a different technology. The new technology would then have it' s own S curve. However there may be instances where it may be possible to 'stretch' the S curve to extend the life cycle of a given technology. Such incremental enhancements, useful as they might be, are generally restricted to a given class (Class I, II or III) (see. Figure 7.2).

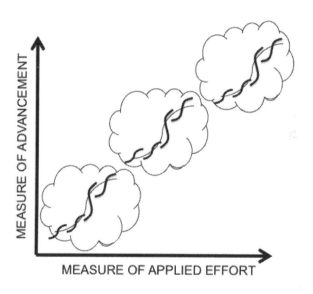

Figure 7.2, Technology S curves within innovation classes

Occasionally however there are instances where it may not make sense to extend the S curve. At that point it probably makes sense to simply abandon a given technology and move to the innovative application. Changes of this type are pioneering in nature, i.e. they tend to change the value proposition of the consumers of an existing technology. When this happens there is usually a discontinuity (or a lag time) between an existing technology and the new technology. The discontinuity poses itself as an opportunity to exploit the marketplace either for introducing a new innovation or creating a new market (Figure 7.2).

As existing technologies develop, companies look to reach more lucrative markets. To do this firms typically target a higher-end consumer. At the same time, companies often lose sight of their less profitable customers, those in the more budget conscious range. This happens because to satisfy their high-end customers companies often improve on their existing technology to the point that results in a "performance oversupply." Because of the improvements, the most basic product model typically becomes more expensive, and the capabilities far exceed those demanded by others. Because the lower end customers do not need all of the expensive innovations that the firm has invested so heavily in, they often do not want to pay for them. This leaves a window of opportunity for pioneering technologies to gain a foothold. When this happens a "Price-Value" gap exists. This creates a group of disenfranchised consumers who are willing to switch to a new technology that provides fewer benefits but is more affordable. If the entry of a pioneering technology to a market is timed correctly, disenfranchised customers may suddenly switch to the new technology in large numbers. This window of opportunity exists typically when an incremental technology is approaching its maturity stage. Furthermore the incumbent company efforts are focused on maximizing the difference between cost and profits by offering value added features to the least price conscious consumers. At this stage of incremental technology the introduction of the new, inventive technology provides the highest opportunity for success (see figure 7.3).

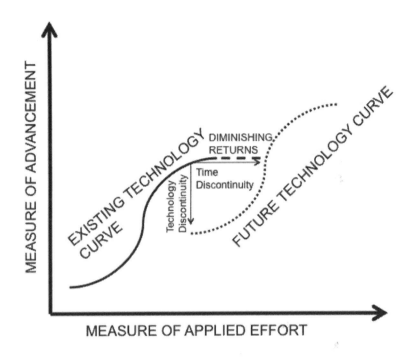

Figure 7.3, Technology and time discontinuities

In an ideal sense, the best time for an innovation to sustain itself is when it's entry is able to capitalize on the *time* and *technology* discontinuities. Good leaders therefore are those that have an eye for identifying such discontinuities. Therefore, a distinctive competence for a leader is to have an ability to spot opportunities to innovate. Clearly this occurs when the organizational context facilitates nurturing of such skills, besides the existence of business processes to ensure effective articulation (Dhillon 2008).

Examples of Incremental Innovations

As discussed previously, incremental innovations within the focused market are those that help in providing a better product or a service within a narrow scoped market. An example of this type of improvement could be when Great Plains accounting software package (since acquired by Microsoft), which allows for customized reports for businesses added the functionality improvement of allowing managers to perform forecasting and budgeting reports. This improvement is beneficial to those seeking a customized accounting package. However it does not change their value perspective on the product/service being offer by Great Plains.

Incremental innovations within the universal market are those that help in providing a better product or a service, which can be applied to a broad group of customers. An example of this type of innovative improvement is when Virginia based Code Blue Solutions provided their customers with an opportunity to link their Electronic Medical Records software, Catalis, with their medical billing company to ensure that the physician's are charging properly for the all the procedures they performed during an office visit. This type of improvement allows all physicians using the Catalis system the ability to increase their efficiency and accuracy which is already part of the value perspective they have towards EMR systems.

Incremental innovations within the mass market are those that help in providing a better product or a service, which can be applied to a range of customers. An example of an incremental improvement in this class is when Amazon added a feature to their website allowing customers to view multiple used books being offered by individuals and thus providing them an ability to comparative shop between the different book sellers based on the price and condition quality of the books being offered for sale. While this feature improvement is well appreciated by their customers it is still within the value perspective of consumers who are engaged in transactions within E-markets.

Examples of pioneering innovations

Pioneering innovations are those innovations that help facilitate a change from one class to another and thereby changing the value perspective in the process. An example of such innovations may be represented by Earnest & Young's creation of an Internet-based service for tax consulting in the early 1990's. With $6000 annual subscription fee, it enabled small and medium sized businesses to access nearly 20,000 tax and accounting consultants. Such cost effective efficiency gains are clearly improvements that the current customers value and help in improving the product and services while moving the value perspective from the focused class to the universal class.

Another example of a pioneering innovation is the technology, which enabled the brokerage firm Charles Schwab to offer their financial services online. Initially Charles Schwab was a discount brokerage firm who offered limited services to their clients through an integrated web of brokers, which allowed them to provide their services at a heavily discounted price through a standardized service product. When they entered the online brokerage market competing with the like of E-trade and Ameritrade they were able to capitalize existing customers while offering innovative technologies to those customers who were changing their value perspective from a universal class to a E-market class. This allowed them gain market share rapidly even though they were considered laggards compared to the first movers of E-trade and Ameritrade because of the perception of legitimacy associated with the being a brokerage firm prior to the other online brokerage players.

Leadership competencies and innovation

Ability to recognize the maturity level of a technology
Clearly it is important for an organization's leadership to inculcate an ability to recognize the maturity level of a technology. It is possible to do so by developing an understanding or current organizational structures and ensuring that adequate resources exist for such an activity. At the same time it is also important to establish well defined business process that systematically evaluate and review the current status of the technology in use. A combination of appreciation of organizational structures and processes facilities the development of such a competence. This ability allows management to be proactive in understanding the limitations of current technologies and develop staff to maximize returns from growth technologies.

Ability to understand the nature and scope of technology discontinuities. A technology gap between the current and future functionality exists between an organizations' current technology and a future technology option is know as technology discontinuities. An important component for an Organization's leadership is to continuously stay informed about the available technology trends and technology requirements of the organization. This technology domain knowledge is achieved through the development of a cultural environment, which rewards individuals for constantly scanning the technology field and seeking avenues to develop current knowledge about pioneering technologies. This understanding and appreciation of technology discontinuities allows management to minimize productivity loses due to inefficiencies in the implementation of a new technology.

Ability to understand timeframes for diminishing returns as they relate to barriers. It is very important for an organization to have an understanding of the organizational value being created by technology. As a technology moves along its' lifecycle, the closer it becomes to being obsolete the fewer benefits are

164

contributed to the organization value. A challenge for leaders is to have the prudence to change from one technology to the next at just the right moment in time to minimize the effect of diminishing returns. When executing correctly a progression from one technology to the next generation technology, it could act as a technology barrier for new market entrants because it reduces the likelihood of a disruptive technology entering the market space. This ability provides an organization with a core competence, which could be exploited to gain a competitive advantage.

Ability to understand the strengths and weaknesses of incremental technologies. It is very important for leaders of an organization to periodically assess how well the current technology is meeting their organization's needs as well as those of their customers. It is essential that management knows what their customer's expectations are and that they know how to match product and service offerings that mirror their customer's needs and expectations. Often this can be achieved through the use of incremental technologies, which offer improvements of their business processes through minor technology improvements or adjustments. A key leadership skill is being able deliver these process improvements. In order to do this it is important to understand the strengths and weaknesses of an organizations current technologies being used as well as those of alternative technologies available to the organization. Being able to select the best combination (portfolio) of technologies to deliver the desired benefits is a management competence, which can help strengthen the relationships between an organization and their customers. This type of relationship builds a trusting relationship and a loyal customer base with a higher level of switching cost which is a also considered a barrier to entry for new entrants in the market.

Ability to recognize pioneering technologies that could provide opportunities or pose threats. Additionally, it is important for management to consider the treats or opportunities that exist within the new pioneering technologies that are becoming available within the organization's industry. It is critical for all organizations to continuously scan their industry's technology trends and to identify opportunities to improve their organization's performance from pioneering technologies before a their competitors are able to get a significant first mover advantage on them. It is important to note that not all emerging technologies will offer the same value proposition to an organization and their customers. However, to be able to effectively lead an organization through the current global market, leaders need to have the ability to recognize those pioneering technologies with the potential to change the value proposition of the users.

Summary

This chapter has showed innovative technology as a key ingredient for delivering superior performance for an organization. We present a framework that conceptualizes the nature and scope of *incremental* and *pioneering* innovations. Our characterization of innovation progression within a market setting, helps in identifying and defining mechanisms for establishing leadership strategies, that guide an organization to successfully incorporate a given innovation within their targeted market group. We have discussed how IT applications have the potential to lower costs or create differentiation across a wide array of activities in a firm's value chain through the introduction and use of either incremental or pioneering innovations. A strategic leadership competence is the ability to understand and appreciate the strategic use of IT and to consider future options affecting the way an organization works. Having an understanding of the potential strategic impact of incremental and pioneering innovations as well as how they are integrated with business processes are leadership skills can lead to the development of a sustainable competitive advantage for an organization.

8. IT and Social Responsibility

There is no doubt that information technology has permeated all aspects of our lives – from booking flights to buying insurance and getting a home mortgage. Not only can most tasks be carried out without speaking to a single person, they are based on highly automated electronic systems. The way in which information technology has permeated our lives also questions our values, morals and responsibilities. Would we indeed like computers to take control of our lives? Would we like to let go of our personal private space? Can we really trust the electronic systems for their reliability and quality of information they produce? What about an array of freedom of speech, property right and ownership issues? All these questions are important ones to consider and are discussed in this chapter.

Accessibility to technology

Accessibility to technology is a growing concern, for different societies. Not only there are disparities between the economically advantaged and disadvantaged countries, there are also significant inequalities within individual countries. Such inequalities might arise as a consequence of gender, race or simply the economic status of some societies. Clearly there are some groups that are more disadvantages than others – low-income persons living in rural areas, young and single parent families. In his book *The new barbarian manifesto*, Ian Angell (2000) has argued that advances in information and communication technologies are in fact fostering divisions in society and as a consequence are widening the gap between those who "have" and those who "have not". Such disparities can be observed not only within countries, but also at a global scale.

Researchers tend to present differing viewpoints as to the consequences of varying levels of access to technology. There are a group of researchers who seem to feel that advances in information and communication technologies, and Internet in particular, are going to decrease the divide between those who have access to technology and those who do not. The first argument, as maintained by Ian Angell, (1996) is that technological divide will give rise to a 'new barbarian' and there is bound to be a lot of turmoil in the information age. Reich (1992) and Ohmae (1995) resonate somewhat with this view in their claim that in years to come we will see an emergence of the 'symbolic-analyst', who could be construed as 'information rich' and the others who would be 'information poor'. Ohmae (1995) makes an economic argument to propose that *inter linked economies* are the organizing logic of the future as opposed to nation states. To a large extent this is abetted by the convergence of information and communication technologies. In many ways this dispiriting future is here. Dhillon et al (2001) illustrate this phenomena by presenting a review of networked firms operating in an *inter linked economy* and the challenges that a developing country faces.

There is some merit is postulating the negative consequences of information technology advent and increased divide between groups of people. For instance, in the wealthiest nations, there are

31,046 Internet hosts per million inhabitants while for the poorest nations there are only 9 per million inhabitants. In the mid 1990s International Telecommunication Union has reported that more than 90% households in high-income countries have a telephone line and in some cases have more than one, but in comparison only 2% of households in low-income countries have the service. It is also estimated that out of 950 million households in the world, 65% of the total do not have a telephone. Situation has marginally improved with respect to fixed telephony. However mobile technologies change the context a bit. And we are witnessing rapid changes at the moment. Access to telephone service is not only a good indicator of a country's telecommunications infrastructure, but also a suitable gauge of the level of access to information. This suggests that there is clearly a significant level of disparity between those who have access to information and those who do not, which perhaps could have negative consequences for the society at large.

The second argument, as contended by Burn and Loch (2001) is that the Internet will help in closing the divide between the have and have-nots. Burn and Loch give the example of Egypt where a model of technology diffusion was developed that includes education and training, infrastructure, and IT. The applications developed in Egypt were both culturally and socially appropriate so as to gain widespread acceptance. Although education and training have been argued as cornerstones of realizing a technological diffusion, the benefits derived could be marginal since a majority of the populace may not have access to even basic education. Clearly as with any technological innovation majority of the benefits reside in the related changes.

Property rights and ownership issues

Intellectual property and ownership are crucial issues in the information age. Software piracy remains one of the foremost intellectual property right issues, and yet a complex one.

Although monetary losses because of software piracy in the US have been significant ($34 billion for 2013. In 1996 it was 13 billion) the software piracy rates when compared with rest of the world are rather modest. The Software and Information Industry Alliance (SIIA) has however reported a decline in software piracy in 1999 to $11 billion. The 1994 figures from Business Software Alliance estimate US software piracy rate at 35%. Although Europe has the highest overall piracy rate, piracy in Asia costs the software industry highest in monetary terms. The Hong Kong piracy rate is almost double that of the US (with an average of 72%). Hong Kong and China perhaps pose a very serious threat to the software industry. It has been estimated that there are some 26 'factories' in China that produce some 75 million pirated compact discs each year. The local market absorbs less than 1% of the total production. These copies are often smuggled to Latin American and European countries.

Numerous studies have been conducted to explain reasons behind software piracy. These have ranged from ease of theft and people's sense of proportional value to cost, censure and availability as the main drivers Moores and Dhillon (2000). The SIIA has vehemently argued that since software piracy is an illegal act, the associated activities of buying and selling are also illegal and hence makes calls for increased legislation and enforcement. Although SIIA explains the decline in software piracy between 1994 and 1998 simply in terms of cost, cost *per se* does not seem to figure in SIIA's drive in managing piracy. This suggests that perhaps software developers are charging more than necessary for the software. One reason could be the near monopolistic environment in which most companies operate.

There are also researchers who argue (e.g. Weckert, 1996) that unauthorized copying is not morally wrong, except when its morally wrong to act illegally. Weckert poses three scenarios to make his point. First, where an individual may copy software just for evaluation, with the intent of buying it if it proves to be satisfactory. Second, where an individual copies a game, but would never buy it because he thinks it's not worth doing so. Third, where an individual copies software for commercial gain and if the software was not available for copying, the individual would buy it. According to Weckert, clearly the owner of the software is harmed in the third case. Based on these assertions Weckert contends that copying is certainly not immoral and that a case against copying ought to be firmly established before restrictions are put in place.

There are various other viewpoints on software piracy and intellectual property rights. Swinyard, et al. (1990), for example, argue that the notion of copyright is a Western concept and that for the Asians becoming skilled means to copy the master. Therefore the authors contend that high piracy rates in Asia are a cultural issue with individuals viewing software piracy relative to potential benefits to self, family and community. Conner and Rumelt (1991) argue that existence of pirated software is actually beneficial to software developers since it draws people into the software market and also is a means to distribute 'free' copies to potential customers, who otherwise might not be aware.

Freedom of speech issues

Aspects of freedom of speech have always been of concern to a broad cross section of the populace. Even today freedom of speech issues are hotly contested. Only recently there were a lot of feelings expressed with the destruction of Buddha's statues in Afghanistan. Such occurrences have always been the musings of scholars and theologians alike. However with the recent advent of technology and the Internet, freedom of speech issues seem to have become of interest to the public.

In the United States the First Amendment to the Constitution (Freedom of Speech) has always acted as a shield between citizen and the government. Individual States have tried to enact legislation to 'criminalize' the intentional transmission of 'obscene and indecent' messages but it has been rather difficult to define what constitutes 'obscene' or 'indecent'. Some headway was made in the 1996 Communication Decency Act where 'obscene' and 'indecent' are defined as the transmission of information which depicts or describes 'sexual or excretory activities or organs' in a manner deemed 'offensive' by community standards. However understanding and regulating 'community standards' in the cyberspace is not only difficult, but also subjected to standards of the most restrictive communities in the nation. The act was challenged (and lost) on grounds that it violated the First Amendment insofar as that it caused 'blanket restriction' of free speech. The act also failed to define 'indecent' adequately. Although this was an attempt by the moral leaders to manage content on the Internet, at the same time it was a victory for those who supported free speech over the Internet.

Sex sites are not the only sites that are under fire. Hate speeches, online stalking and 'recipe books' for terrorist groups are also of concern. As Warren and Hutchinson (2001) suggests, today a number of terrorist groups are using the Internet to further their cause. Prominent among these are the Zapatista Movement web site detailing their struggle against the Mexican authorities and TamilNet, the voice of the Tamil Tigers. Many terrorists groups not only use the Internet to raise funds, disseminate information, they are also using information and communication technologies to engage in denial of service and even direct attacks. For instance the Portuguese hacker group, PHAIT (Portuguese Hackers Against Indonesian Tyranny) rewrote a number of Indonesian government and commercial web sites to protest about East Trimor (as quoted in Warren and Hutchinson, 2001).

There are two viewpoints regarding such 'bad speech' on the Internet. First, and the most obvious, is to strictly regulate the traffic. Such an action, however, comes under attack from the proponents of freedom of speech. Second, that the pursuit of truth is best served by allowing all kinds of views to be presented in the 'market of ideas'. The inherent contention is that only by free discussion of ideas and arguments will the real truth emerge (Elgesem, 1996).

Quality and reliability of information and systems

Issues of quality and reliability of information and the related systems have perhaps received the most attention. Earlier work on quality of information was essentially carried out by software engineers (Boehm et al, 1979; McCall, 1979). The software engineers tried to describe quality of software by identifying series of attributes. Attributes in turn would have more attributes. Identifications and description of such attributes helped in formulating a set of quality characteristics that could help in defining system specification and help in simplifying the quality assurance process. This earlier work went a long way in developing quality practices and in laying down the foundation for present day software metrics. In recent years a number of additional best practices and codes have been developed. Adherence to such codes helps in enhancing system reliability.

Quality attributes were also pivotal in defining good and bad, ethical and unethical software engineering practices. For instance the software development practices followed in commissioning Therac-25 machines in mid 1980s was criticized because basic software quality attributes had not been considered. Therac-25 was a computerized radiation therapy machine, where software from the earlier Therac-6 and Therac-20 had been reused. Following the death of six patients between 1985 and 1987, a number of social responsibility issues were raised. In the Therac-25 case the specialist machine operator upon whom the patients (and the public at large) were relying, did not hone up to their responsibilities. Patients were subjected to repeated radiation doses in spite of the operators knowing that the machines were malfunctioning. The manufacturer was clearly negligent in relation to this treatment equipment, from the original design stage through the much overdue safety renovations. The developers mistakenly believed that taking pieces from various proven machines would create a likewise successful new machine. This was a serious flaw in system design. More importantly, though, the priorities in system quality were poorly arranged with simplicity of use threatening safety. There is a level of social responsibility (even greater in a industry such as medicine) that companies are entrusted with as we proceed into an era of all consuming technology. The developers would have been far better off to meet those responsibilities proactively rather than reactively.

In recent years the social responsibility issues related to quality and reliability of information and the related systems have been repeatedly questioned. When the London Ambulance computer aided dispatch system failed in 1992; who was to blame? London Ambulance, presumably the largest in the world covering over 600 square miles and a resident population of nearly seven million, carries over 5000 patients and receives between 2000 and 2500 calls per day. But numerous problems related to contractor selection, planning, project management and implementation resulted in complete failure of the computer-based system. The inquiries that ensued found that the system did not meet functionality or performance criteria and much of the design had fatal flaws that would, and did, cumulatively lead to all of the symptoms of system failure. This resulted in lengthy response times, numerous callbacks, and a large wait time to speak with a dispatcher.

When systems as critical as Therac-25 and London Ambulance fail, there are obviously social responsibility concerns. Clearly lack of quality in systems analysis, design and management results are the root causes. Ultimately, as observed by Bowen (2000), "it is unethical to develop software for safety-related systems without following the best practice available". As a matter of fact it is unethical to develop software for any kind of a system, may it be safety-critical or not. By following unethical information systems project management best practices, the baggage handling systems of the Chek Lap Kok airport in Hong Kong and Denver airport in the US resulted in disasters. The Nevada, California and Oregon Department of Motor Vehicle systems had a similar fate because corners were cut and basic guidelines for software development and project management were not followed.

Aspects of a viable social responsibility program

The previous sections have identified and addressed a broad range of social responsibility issues, which if ignored are going to result in some ethical strain. In the paragraphs below, based on an understanding of potential ethical strains, key elements of a viable social responsibility program are identified and described.

Socially responsible individual practice

As has been noted elsewhere, even law and regulatory frameworks call upon individuals to engage in some sort of 'self regulation'. However, prior to expecting individuals to self regulate, it is not only important to make them aware of the various issues, but also train, and motivate them to consider various social responsibility issues.

In a research paper, Dhillon (2001), while discussing violations of safeguards by trusted personnel notes that had individuals within Barings Bank been aware and well trained to be socially responsible, the demise of the 223 year old merchant bank could have been prevented. Since various groups of individuals within the bank lacked the ability to recognize patterns related to abuse of position and circumvention of organizational and technological controls, they failed to recognize any mis-dealings on part of Nicholas Leeson, the accused.

In a similar vein, if an average user of technology is not made aware of the manner in which various Internet businesses infringe the right to individual privacy, they would not be able to even recognize if any transgression has taken place. Such an issue is more important today than ever before, since concrete laws either do not exist or are still in the process of being defined.

Ethical systems development

Given that majority of IT implementations within organizations result in failure or inappropriate use, there is a need to consider the ethical aspects of the systems development process. Consider the recent Nevada Department of Motor Vehicle's (DMV) systems development fiasco. The goal was to implement one stop shopping for drivers' licenses and registration, Internet and telephone transactions, registration at smog check stations, and of course, the reduction of abnormally long waiting times. This was to be achieved using a $35 million computer system that was, unfortunately, not implemented skillfully; full of bugs and slower than expected; it certainly did not help the backlog that DMV was struggling with initially. In months subsequent to the implementation failure, the bugs were removed and the system improved, albeit at a cost. However low employee morale and high turnover besides a bothered public are some of the legacies left behind. Yet the new system at the branch level is not much easier, and not any quicker, than the old.

At the heart of the DMV's problem with the computer system, is not so much a technological issue, but a shear lack of ethical standards and inadequate social responsibility. Clearly a lack of good management - poor planning and design undermined the good intentions. The political (and contractual) constraints on time and staffing, as well as other problems that come with being a state agency, set the stage for a "mission impossible". Still, the legislature believed two consultants were up to the task, and for enough money they took it on. These are ethical and social responsibility IT project management issues that clearly need to be adequately understood.

There are several issues that contributed to the poor implementation, untimely completion, and unsatisfactory result of the DMV computer system. Among these is poor project management, the confusing role of two consultants, non-replaced downtime of existing employees for training and other human resource matters. As has been argued elsewhere (e.g. see Wood-Harper, et al, 1996; Rahanu, et al,1996) such issues could have been rectified by focusing on project management and systems development ethics. Clearly the system analysts had a social responsibility to elicit the right requirements, systems developers the responsibility to design a system to fit the needs of the current environment and project managers the responsibility to meet stakeholder expectations.

Establishing responsibilities

The call to establish responsibility structures can best be described by considering the context of the Therac-25, a computerized radiation therapy machine briefly mentioned in the previous section. This machine had been built after the Therac-6 and the Therac-20 models, originally developed in the early 1970's. The Therac-25 was considered more compact, more versatile and possibly more user friendly then the previous two models. The Therac-25 had some software that was reused from the Therac-6 and Therac-20 but it eliminated the use of some of the hardware previously used. Because the Therac-25 took advantage of the computer's abilities to control and monitor the hardware, it was decided not to duplicate all the safety mechanisms and interlocks that the previous models used. The manufacturer, perhaps to cut the expenses, removed the hardware interlocks and backups thus putting more faith on software. There were eleven Therac-25's installed in the US and Canada in 1985. Between 1985 and 1987, six accidents involving massive overdoses to patients occurred. In 1987 the Therac-25 was recalled so that not only the software could be corrected but also the machines could be redesigned to include hardware safeguards against software errors. During this recall, it was discovered that related problems existed in the Therac-20 software.

This case calls forth numerous questions about responsibility and liability related to modern technology. More specifically, given the medical use of the technology in this case, questions of professional standards and ethical codes are raised. It seems all too often, as with this case, consumers (or patients) find themselves nowadays in a state of "buyer beware". But as the patient or the consumer, is this really your responsibility? It is completely unreasonable to expect that individuals in need of radiation therapy would have in depth knowledge (or bear the time and cost to obtain it) regarding all the medication and equipment that will be inflicted upon them. Clearly in the Therac case the specialist upon which the patients (and the public at large) were relying, did not hone up to their responsibilities. The manufacturer was clearly negligent in relation to this treatment equipment, from the original design stage through the much overdue safety renovations. The manufacturer mistakenly believed that taking pieces from various proven machines would create a likewise successful new machine. This was a serious flaw in system design. More importantly, though, the priorities in system quality were poorly arranged with simplicity of use threatening safety. There is a level of social responsibility that companies are entrusted with as we proceed into an era of all consuming technology. The manufacturer would have been far better off to meet those responsibilities proactively rather than reactively. As a manufacturer, however, the company is not held to any professional ethics like doctors themselves.

Another question that arises is to ask where the governmental agencies should step in? Although it is true the Therac-25 was saving many lives in the same period in which it took some, and irreparably damaged others. The manufacturer, however, being previously negligent in their responsibilities should not have been instructed (and entrusted) to notify the users. The FDA should have taken the notification actions itself. While the two exchanged meaningless correspondence about what the users should be told, more patients were harmed. The FDA's likewise reactive approach also leaves a lot to be desired. The agency should be far more proactive in regulating the initial release of equipment, than ambulance chasing later to find enough faults for recall or required renovations.

In this case the middlemen, the technicians, are not without some responsibility. Taking a carefree and resigned approach as they did to using machinery of this magnitude was erroneous on their part. Machines should never have been told to proceed as many as 5 times after malfunctioning, or patients segregated from the technician in such a manner that they could not be seen or heard. The continued use through the day of malfunctioning equipment is troubling at best.

It is therefore important to understand and establish adequate responsibility structures. It may be prudent to delineate the roles when say a new technology is introduced or a change is made in the functionality. Not only is it important to identify high level stakeholders, so as to influence current and future policy initiatives, but also to establish stakeholders at an operational level so as to have identifiable incumbents where the buck would stop. Such individuals would obviously have to be empowered. In the Therac case, had the technicians been empowered to take a decision not to use the machines, a number of tragedies could have been prevented. Another important issue related to empowerment is that of training, which would enable individuals to recognize that a problem exists in the first place.

Instituting training programs

Besides a lack of planning, inadequate training is perhaps an important reason for failure of IT implementations (Martocchio, 1992). Any organization is socially obliged and is responsible for training end users to manage technology. As is evident from a number of case studies, lack of training has a knock on effect on customer service, employee morale and increased incidents of crime and fraud.

In the Nevada DMV case discussed above, besides other reasons, inability of the organization to institute well thought through training programs resulted in an organization failing to capitalize on the technology. Since a DMV system services the needs of a large proportion of the population, one could argue that the organizations failed to uphold its social responsibility. Similar instances of lack of training and inability of the employees and end users to understand and appreciate corporate change initiatives can be found in IT implementations at the Oregon DMV, Californian DMV, the 1992 London Ambulance IT implementation fiasco, to name a few.

What can easily be taken from the above studies and conclusions is that organizations need to take the time to really get to know their employees. Rapid technological change is going to continue into the next decade and unprepared reactive response to that change is not going to be good enough. Organizations need to begin to prepare themselves now by restructuring the human resources and training and development departments of their business. The goal behind this restructuring should be to create a highly skilled, motivated, and self-assured and socially responsible groups of individuals who will be prepared for change when it comes about. Organizations will need to begin to address and improve the issue of low self-efficacy through on-going training courses tailored to the knowledge and confidence level of these associates. These courses should be designed to address the individual areas of concern and increase their self-efficacy prior to the need for new technology training by slowly introducing computer functions at an individual pace. Training should not solely be focused on

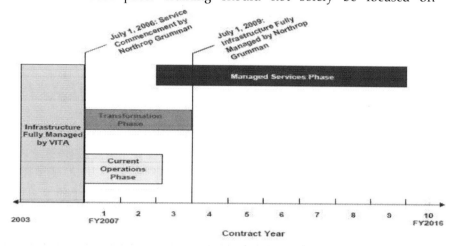

technological aspects, but psychological issues of low self-efficacy should be concentrated on as well. Therefore, motivational training should be a large portion of this undertaking. As Smith-Jentsch, et al (1996) note "pre-training motivation is expected to prepare trainees to learn by heightening their attention and increasing their receptivity to new ideas."

Corporations can no longer afford to let their own employees hinder them from continued growth. Therefore, organizations that can recognize now the need to escort their associates into the future by preparing them ahead of time for inevitable technological changes will be the ones that would be more successful, more ethical and responsible.

End-users need a lesson in ethics

Clearly end-users need a lesson in ethics. This is because business corporations and governments alike have increasingly become dependent on IT. However, we are constantly reminded of spectacular intrusions into supposedly secure computer installations for a variety of illicit purposes, including theft, fraud and sabotage. Such is the concern that international bodies such as the Organizations for Economic Co-operation & Development, the International Chamber of Commerce and the Council of Europe, among others, have focused on the question. In UK the Department of Trade and Industry has also launched several initiatives to address the issue.

While it is clear that business organizations and society at large are directly affected because of their dependence on computers, it is difficult to find reliable figures for monetary loss, and assess the extent of impact. The 1994 UK Audit Commission survey revealed that in the previous three years the total value of cases reported went up by 183%. Figures coming from the US suggest anything up to yearly damages of $2bn could be involved, although something in the region of $145m-$730m seems more realistic.

What may be trivial in its self-evidence but profound in its truth is that prevention of computer related abuse is more effective than treatment. At a societal level, the diffusion of ideas about ethical use of computers as part of the cultural infrastructure could reduce the burden placed on the shoulders of IT managers. Many large organizations are engaging in awareness campaigns that seek to increase understanding of and sensitivity towards misuse/abuse of computers among the broad base of their employees, rather than merely concentrate on those with responsibility for computer systems. There are initiatives being developed seeking to educate youngsters in ethical use of technology as they learn about computers.

Ultimately the need is to have both a higher level of awareness among the workforce generally about the costs and benefits of good ethical practices, and a framework of computer law and enforcement to provide necessary support where the more informal system of checks and balances fails.

Conclusion

Clearly there is a need to understand various aspects of ethical strains and potential social responsibility concerns. Such issues gain significance when the task at hand is of either managing a new technology or introducing innovative technologies into business settings. Mars (1982) for instance notes, "there is only a blurred line between enterpreneuriality and flair on the one hand and sharp practice and fraud on the other". This is indeed an outcome of an ambitious attitude of the society towards many fiddles. Mills [23] portrayed business as operating in a 'subculture of structural immoralities'. Moreover Croall (1992) feels that the 'blurred line' gives ample scope for the offenders to argue that their activities fall on the right side of the line.

Today, management fears computer fraud more than any other kind of fraud. Evidence coming from across the globe indicates that computer related crime afflicts practically all nations, even those we might consider unlikely. For the organizations, the pressing question is how to control this new affliction. One of the cornerstones of control and management of computer crime is a social responsibility framework and ethical principles to adequately protect and manage diverse systems. However control can be implemented at two levels. At a macro level by enacting relevant laws and at a micro level by adopting better management practices. Associated with fears of security and crime are also the issues of reliability and quality, and managers involved in dealing with each of the concerns should give due consideration to the social responsibility challenges. It is our hope that issues identified in this chapter set the tone for setting an agenda that will hone in on social responsibility concerns in the information age.

Case Studies

9. VITA - a muddled affair*

The Executive Summary

For the past few decades, Virginia has tried to consolidate the information technology (IT) functions of state agencies, without avail. Despite past failures, the modernization of the state IT system was absolutely necessary because of the inefficiencies of the old system. Virginia's IT was insecure and disjointed across all agencies.

In 2005, Virginia entered into a $2.3 billion contract with Northrop Grumman (NG) to outsource Virginia's IT system. The contract had a $236 million yearly cap that could be adjusted for inflation and extraordinary expenditures. The transition to the NG managed-service was to occur over a three-phase process. Unfortunately, Northrop Grumman and the Virginia Information Technology Agency (VITA) encountered problems nearing the end of Phase 1, with incomplete physical inventory cost

* The case was prepared by Khoi Ta, Saa'dia Talbert, Riccardo Terenghi, Peter Thacker, Timothy Tran under the tutelage of Dr. Gurpreet Dhillon

allocation. This delay affected the completion of Phase 2 for the end of June 2009.

Because of the increasing complications and delays, an investigative committee was organized to report on the current progress of the entire outsourcing project. In spite of the additional current benefits resulting from the portion of transition that has already occurred, state agencies discovered that the costs of those benefits were becoming too high. With mounting speculation about the execution of the project, both sides were finding fault with the other side. NG complained that VITA and state agencies were either uncooperative or slow in aiding their physical inventory counting. In addition, NG states that VITA expanded NG's scope beyond the initial contract terms, previously agreed upon.

VITA criticized NG's inability to meet deadlines in a timely or efficient manner. These delays were compounded with doubts among agencies about the monitoring software NG implemented for remote IT management, citing security flaws. In addition, VITA accused NG of improperly allocating costs, and poorly servicing to state agencies.

As of August 28, 2009, NG submitted a Corrective Action Plan to VITA that outlined resolutions to all of the current issues and met the new target date of June 30, 2010. This plan aims to facilitate the transition process with heightened communication channels and a renewed focus on the company's familiarity with Virginia's IT system. These changes are intended to fix previous mistakes in the phase completion.

Despite previous missteps, the fact remains that future action needs to be taken. The current CIO, George Coulter, is taking action to simplify the process with a company-wide reorganization. It seems that the main problem source resides in the area of miscommunication. First and foremost, NG and VITA need to work with each other to ease communication difficulties.

Politically, both sides have taken a specific stance. Republican Bob McDonnell would like to wait for the investigative report to finish, before taking action. Democrat Creigh Deeds has already stated that he will take a more active approach in managing the project, including an extensive audit of VITA's performance.

In any industry, new changes, especially in areas that could drastically affect company culture, are expected to meet challenges and hindrances. What matters is how a company handles and perseveres through complications, especially for changes that are meant to improve the organization's future. Effective change management is needed during this time to bring the stakeholders together for the benefit of the State of Virginia. While the deal had executive government buy-in, many state agencies and their staff who were directly affected by the changes were not on board and therefor are not positively impacted by the NG/VITA partnership.

Introduction & Background

The State has attempted to unify information technology functions across government agencies several times since the 1980's. One such time was when the Department of Information Technology (DIT) was formed to be the master information technology agency. State agencies relied on DIT for information technology and telecommunications needs. This was not a successful venture.

The State attempted once more in 2002 to centralize state government Information Technology across agencies with the formation of the Virginia Information Technologies Agency (VITA). Governor Warner proposed the consolidation of all information technology services and governance after reviewing the Joint Legislative Audit and Review Commission (JLARCS) reports in December 2002.(JLARC) The reports found $75 million in failed information technology projects and $28 million in cost overruns. JLARC recommended the creation of an Information

Technology Investment Board (ITIB) to approve information technology projects for all state agencies. In addition, they recommended that a full-time Chief Information Officer (CIO) be hired to oversee information technology project management. (Interim Review) The CIO would report to the ITIB. The Secretary of Technology stated that, "Governor Warner's reforms would save $100 million in revenues state-wide annually". (JLARC)

As a result, the 2003 General Assembly enacted legislation to create VITA. Per the JLARC Report to the Senate Finance committee, "Existing Information Technology agencies were consolidated, plus most State Agencies. While 'out-of-scope' agencies were not consolidated, including higher education and the Port Authority." (JLARC) The consolidations only affected infrastructure and State Agencies maintained operation of all other information technology . Enterprise infrastructure, i.e. hardware, personal computers and servers, became the responsibility of VITA. In addition, support staff was consolidated. Agency specific infrastructure (traffic-light management or point-of-sale systems), enterprise applications (CARS & CIPPS), and agency specific applications (Medicaid or offender management systems) all stayed with the respective state agency. (JLARC)

In addition the 2003 Legislation reformed information technology governance. The Information Technology Investment Board was created and was statutorily responsible for 'planning, budgeting, acquiring, using, disposing, managing, and administering information technology. The ITIB has nine voting members plus the Auditor of Public Accounts (APA). The CIO is responsible for creating a unified approach to information technology for State agencies. Finally, the CIO and VITA have the following oversight responsibilities: they have sole statutory authority to procure information technology goods and services and manage IT contracts. The Project Management Division must provide consulting support and oversight for IT projects. (JLARC).

VITA's mission is, "To provide information technology that enables government to better serve the public. Their vision is 'to be Virginia's preferred government IT partner.'" (VITA website) VITA has the following five core goals:

- Create value; Provide enterprise IT services supporting the business of state government at the best return on investment for our customers, stakeholders and Virginia's taxpayers.

- Improve the Commonwealth's competitive position in the national and world marketplace; Harness opportunities to utilize technology to improve the availability, quality and responsiveness of state services- seamless, friendly, anywhere, anytime; for our citizens and customers.

- Create accountability for how public funds are spent on technology for VITA as well as for the entire executive branch.

- Grow our employees; Embed opportunities for professional growth and development into the agency's organization and operations. Recognize and reward accomplishments.

- Serve as the model for transforming state government; Pursue streamlined business processes and innovative partnerships that revolutionize service delivery at significantly lower costs.

Per VITA's website their organizational structure emphasizes customer service and promotes consistent technological competence and opportunities for professional advancement. Underneath the Chief Information Officer of the Commonwealth, VITA is organized into eleven directorates, with six functional leads for reporting and planning purposes. (VITA website)

Partnership Contract & Implementation Strategy

In 2005 the State of Virginia entered into a contract with Northrop Grumman with the goal of modernizing its infrastructure. This public-private partnership contract allowed a 10 year span for the completion of the transition; however, the two parties recognized this past August that the project is about nine months behind the original schedule. The contract was signed for $2.3 billion with a payment cap of $236 million a year that can be adjusted yearly for inflation and extraordinary IT expenditures. The private party is expected to transform the IT infrastructure of 91 executive branch agencies of the Commonwealth of Virginia. As reported on Northrop Grumman website's, "IT services provided by the infrastructure partnership will include network services, desktop services and e-mail, data-center consolidation and management, customer-care services, call centers, and other infrastructure projects and services."

The contract states that the transition to a managed-services environment has to occur in three distinct phases between 2006 and 2009. Under the managed-services environment, Northrop Grumman will still be responsible for providing hardware, software, facilities, and assistance; however, when NG will fully manage Virginia's IT infrastructure the payments will be based on volume of services used (almost like a fee for the right to use the infrastructure). The VITA-NG partnership is considered by many to be a pioneering approach to IT outsourcing because Virginia was the first state to adopt such a model for IT operations and governance in the entire United States. The partnership represents the most comprehensive information technology reform in the nation and establishes Virginia as a leader in the use of technology in government. It was reported in Information Week (6/19/2009) that, "the IT infrastructure partnership is a visionary, groundbreaking concept never undertaken before. The partnership is addressing much more than IT. It is helping Virginia foster significant organizational and cultural changes within state government to improve efficiency and service delivery."

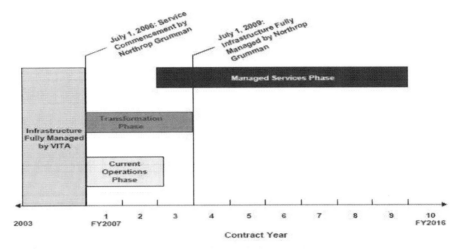

Figure 9.1: Transformation to a Managed Service Environment Occurs in Three Phases (Source: Comprehensive Infrastructure Agreement Detailed Transition Plan (June 2005)

The modernization of the State's IT was necessary because the old system was antiquated and inefficient. It was not secure, uneven in quality, and fragmented from agency to agency. Reformation of hardware, software, and services was necessary to improve operations, support, and maintenance of the system. Upon completion of the modernization and the passage to a managed-services environment, Northrop Grumman will provide specific services such as:

- construction of two new data centers to deliver infrastructure services to the State, including leasing office space to the State in the primary data center located in Chester;

- disaster recovery services to protect the State's "mission critical" applications;

193

- information security services that include the physical protection of IT assets as well as protection from electronic threats such as viruses;

- regular replacement of the State's IT infrastructure, including desktops, laptops, and servers;

- a single help desk to support the State's IT functions.

The transition to a fully managed-services environment will occur in three phases, each phase describes the timeline of operations and the obligations and terms that both VITA and Northrop Grumman have to respect.

Phase one is known as "Current Operations Phase." It lasted two full years from July 1, 2006, to June 30, 2008, and included both one time activities and services to be provided throughout the life of the partnership. In this phase, Northrop Grumman built two new data centers, the customer help desk, and began taking an inventory of the assets at VITA. A final asset inventory is necessary to determine a resource based fee for technology usage, which will determine the payments in the services-managed environment. In this phase, NG started being in charge of managing the State's servers and providing daily assistance to employees in dealing with personal computers issues.

Phase two is called "Transformation Phase" and started on July 1, 2006, with the service commencement by Northrop Grumman. This phase was scheduled to end on June 30, 2009, but currently it has not been completed. As of August 2009, six milestones out of 74 still needed to be completed; the new deadline for their completion and the passage to a fully private managed environment is March 2010. The main goal of this phase is to completely replace the IT infrastructures of the State, which entails 91 agencies spread across about 2,200 locations.

The last phase is the "Managed Services Phase." It started at the beginning of the third year of contract, on July 1, 2008. Despite implementation of the "Transformation Phase" not being completed, Northrop Grumman is able to provide the Commonwealth with independently managed staff, hardware, software, and facilities. This phase will last until the termination of the contract in 2016. If the contract will not be renewed, NG is required to transfer all the tangible assets to the State. The entire physical infrastructure used by the company in the provision of IT services must be transferred at no additional costs.

Problems have existed since the early stages of the partnership. Both sides reported issues that contributed to delays and shift of deadline for the passage to a fully private services-managed environment. While some aspects such as disaster recovery and security, the VITA help desk, and the replacement of computers have led to positive results and satisfaction; others have been delayed and don't provide the expected benefits. Responsibilities are to be shared between both sides; Paul McDougall of Information Week argues that, "progress has been delayed because of inadequate planning by the partnership and a reported reluctance by some agencies to allow transformation to occur." (InformationWeek, Aug 31, 2009) At the time of this paper, 12 agencies still do not enjoy the benefits of the privately managed environment and desktop replacement is not completed in several locations.

A task that Northrop Group failed to complete at this time is the final inventory of all IT structures in the Commonwealth of Virginia. This task is required by the contract and it is a necessary step in the transition to the resource unit billing method to be used in the services-managed environment. Also, NG had to change its initial approach to the transformation of IT resources for the numerous agencies: the company is now transforming one agency at the time and then moving to another agency, instead of transforming one service at the time across all agencies as done in the early years.

Other factors that caused delays include the poor coordination and cooperation of some agencies with Northrop Grumman. Coordination is crucial when changes happen in ongoing businesses; the transition to new systems had to happen smoothly without interfering with the agencies operations, whether they are day-to-day tasks or special projects. Some agencies and staff have shown a general reluctance and hostility towards change and the private partner.

The outsourcing of the IT infrastructure and services for the numerous agencies of the State was intended to improve efficiency of the system, security of the information, better coordination across branches, and avoidance of future costs. The system in place today is definitely more secure and more efficient than the previous system, but the cost avoidance component of the contract has not been achieved. Agencies expected savings from the partnership, but expenditures for many have increased since the commencement of the contract in 2006.

Initial structural changes have been extremely costly; however, analysts predict that significant expenses will be avoided in the future since Northrop Grumman will be responsible for updating the technology, replacing hardware and software, and dealing with technology problems. Cost avoidance is different than savings; operations will not become significantly cheaper. Cost savings may be obtained if the partnership is renewed for three extra years after 2016. This possibility is present in the contract and if the contract is extended VITA's payments to Northrop Grumman will be sensibly lower given the same level of resources usage (see figure 9.2).

During the past two years, there have been many complaints regarding the implementation of the contract with Northrop Grumman and the Company's overall performance. The contract with Northrop Grumman has not resulted in cost savings as originally planned, and, in fact, there has been talk that the contract needs to be renegotiated so that more money is paid to

Northrop Grumman for the same previously agreed upon services. George F. Coulter, the new Chief Information Officer for VITA, has not ruled out that Northrop Grumman would not be prevented from receiving the additional funds it is seeking (Shapiro 09/22/08). According to a recently released document due the Freedom of Information Act, Northrop Grumman was suggesting in April that costs to the state could increase by $26 million per year if changes are not made (Meola 07/25/09).

Table 12: Savings May Result in Last Three Years If the State Extends the Contract

Anticipated Annual Contractual Payments to Northrop Grumman ($ millions)					
Year 3	Year 4	Year 5	Year 6	Years 7-10	Years 11-13
$207.6	$213.5	$203.3	$203.3	$203.2	$175.7

Source: VITA staff analysis of Attachments 10.1.3 - 10.1.5 of Schedule 10.1 of the Comprehensive Infrastructure Agreement as of December 2, 2008.

Figure 9.2, Savings in Last Three Years 2008-2009 Problems

It seems that most of the problems stem from the fact that Northrop Grumman has not been able to accurately identify the information technology assets of the state agencies that it is supposed to administer. Northrop Grumman performed five inventories in order count all of relevant information technology equipment. It is estimated that there are more than 200,000 pieces of equipment at 2,000 sites that Northrop Grumman will need to account for in order know how much VITA should bill state agencies and whether Northrop Grumman is upholding its part of the contract (Bacque 12/14/08). James F. McGuirk II, Chairman of the State Information Technology Investment Board, has said, "We've had several discussions with the head of Northrop Grumman about the ineptness of their inventory. I walk into a room and see 10 [personal computers], I should be able to count to 10 and two weeks later when you ask has how many PCs were in the room, I should be able to tell you

10" (Meola and Ress 07/14/09). According to the Auditor of Public Accounts, a state agency, the inventories that have been performed have errors and the numbers change from month to month (JLARC Report 06/29/09).

Another problem encountered is that Northrop Grumman has not been meeting its deadlines. VITA has granted deadline extensions to Northrop Grumman on more than 40 percent of the key milestones that were supposed to be met. In spite of the extensions, the Company has missed 63 percent of its deadlines. Northrop Grumman has only been early on seven deadlines (Meola and Ress 07/14/09). The Company was to replace 90% of personal computers by March 2009, but as of June less than half had been replaced. The Division of Motor Vehicles, Department of Environmental Quality, and Alcoholic Beverage Commission had none of their computers replaced by the deadline (JLARC Report 06/29/09).

There have been many more problems with the implementation of the contract. Many agencies have doubts about Northrop Grumman's monitoring software, Altiris, that is used to remotely manage IT infrastructure. Consequently, many agencies have resisted using the software because they feel that it could compromise confidential data (JLARC Report 06/29/09). One agency that has resisted using the software is the Virginia State Police; spokeswoman Corinne Geller said, "We have a great deal of sensitive information that we've got to make sure is protected. We're trying to work to ensure that our levels of security are met and [the state IT system's] needs for update and inventory are met" (Bacque 12/14/08).

Audits of the contract with Northrop Grumman have discovered additional problems. Even though Northrop Grumman had been paid by the state for services, the Company was late paying its subcontractors in 40 percent of the cases. Auditors have discovered that Northrop Grumman overcharged the state for personnel costs as compared to what its internal records stated it should be charging in one third of the cases that the auditors tested. This had also been identified as problem during the prior year audit, but was not addressed as the Company had promised to do. Northrop Grumman was charging the state sales tax, even though the original invoices from vendors did not. Although Northrop Grumman stated that it would secure the warehouse where old state computers that may have contained sensitive data were being stored before being erased, Northrop Grumman did not do so (Ress 07/22/09).

Indicative of some of the problems the state is facing over its contract with Northrop Grumman, the total estimated cost over the five-year life of each state laptop computer is $9,000. This equates to $150 per month, of which $26 a month is to cover the cost of replacing a laptop after five years even though the contractor will own the computer (Ress 07/24/09). The state is essentially paying for the same computer twice even though it will never own it. Because when the second five year contract begins for a laptop begins and the state is paying $124 a month ($150 total cost less $26 that is for a future replacment computer), the state has already spent five years paying $26 a month for the same computer, or $1,560 in total. This is in contrast to the $39.33 a month Henrico County pays to lease computers and pay for all support services for its students, Further, Henrico County owns the computers at the end of the leases (Ress 07/24/09).

In an attempt to force Northrop Grumman to improve its service, the Chief Information Officer at the time, Lemuel C. "Lem" Stewart Jr., tried to reduce payments to the Company by 25 percent beginning in March of 2009. Part of the problem was the lack of detail on the invoices submitted by Northrop Grumman and the fact that the Company was almost a year late switching to a billing system that would have provided the information required (Meola and Shapiro 07/28/09). Stewart also tried to withhold payments on bills submitted by Northrop Grumman, but he was overruled on this tactic by the VITA board and was eventually terminated.

Summary of Corrective Action Plan (CAP)

Northrop Grumman is responsible for finishing the project on time and within the budget. However, there were some constraints and dependencies identified by the company prevented it from completing the job before the deadline. First, Northrop Grumman asserted that the Commonwealth had significantly expanded the scope of agency transformation beyond the contract agreement. This expansion required the company to implement transformation within a complex setup of agency-specific cultural and business practice needs far beyond the level of customization contemplated in the contract. Besides, Northrop Grumman had obtained only limited commitment, as well as cooperation from the agencies in a standardized managed infrastructure and support for the transformation. Therefore, the changes by the Commonwealth and agency resistance to the transformation process had resulted in delays and added cost.

To resolve all current issues in the project and to meet the target date of June 30, 2010, Northrop Grumman submitted a Corrective Action Plan to VITA. This plan, dated August 28, 2009, supplements and updates previous versions of the 2006 Detailed Transition Plan from this date forward. This Corrective Action plan outlined several new steps in order to achieve a high-level and comprehensive approach to how Northrop Grumman will cooperatively work with the Commonwealth and its executive agencies, particularly VITA. The company has confidence that this plan can be executed within the schedule it has provided since Northrop Grumman can leverage the lessons learned during the first three years of the project, as well as the increase in familiarity and collaborative work with VITA and the Commonwealth executive agencies. There are particular goals that Northrop Grumman has to accomplish from this plan:

• Northrop Grumman needs to have high degree of coordination with Commonwealth executive agencies and VITA on dates and criteria.

• As the partnership progresses, there has to be substantial progress made to date with performance improving.

• Decision making process and collaboration among all parties in this process have to be improved.

• A new Agency Deployment Manager (ADM) model is implemented to enable direct communication between the agencies and Northrop Grumman managers who are empowered to take quick action and resolve schedule issues.

• A detailed schedule is prepared to show agency dependencies and time for sign-off and acceptance.

• Northrop Grumman understands that it has to finish what is left over in four key components in order to complete the Transition Phase.

Agency Transformations: There are 85 Commonwealth executive agencies from 2,200 locations will be transitioned from their existing infrastructure to the modern, robust infrastructure defined in the Comprehensive Infrastructure Agreement (CIA).

Infrastructure Projects: there are a total of 59 projects that progressively build up IT solutions in the infrastructure used to support system wide managed services. There are 32 of these projects that have been completed, and 28 of them remain in process. The company has defined a set of infrastructure projects which facilitate the successful completion of transition to managed services. The timeline for these projects is illustrated in the figure 9.3.

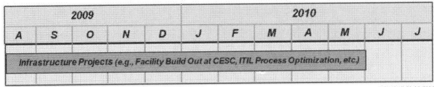

Figure 9.3, Infrastructure Project Timeline

Capstones: these are activities derived from CIA requirements. They are gauge for assessing Northrop Grumman's readiness to provide a managed service to the Commonwealth's agencies. The Capstone project was initiated after the original 2006 Detailed Transition Plan. In this project, VITA prioritized the Capstone items into high, medium, and low priorities. The company plans to accomplish the high priority Capstone items as part of transition. The plan for these high-priority items were presented in two waves. This plan provides a list of Capstone activities associated with transition completion and the evidence needed to demonstrate their completion. Capstone rolling wave planning approach is illustrated as figure 9.4.

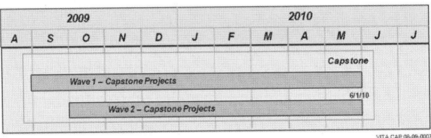

Figure 9.4, Capstone Rolling Wave Planning Approach

The accomplishments of the high-priority items are placed in the Integrated Master Schedule (IMS) as a means of measuring the progress of the transition. Moreover, Northrop Grumman will develop an On-going Operations Plan (OOP) to document its plan to accomplish the medium and low priority Capstone items. The OOP will be delivered to VITA no later than January 1, 2010. The OOP will document the plan to accomplish all medium and low priority Capstone items no later than December 31, 2010.

Milestones in the Comprehensive Infrastructure Agreement (CIA): the CIA milestone provides VITA and the agencies insight into Northrop Grumman's activities as the transition progresses. The CIA Milestones run the duration of the transition phase.

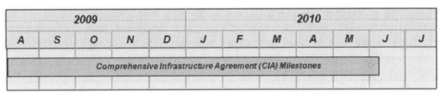

VITA CAP 08-09-0008

Figure 9.5, Milestone Timeline

At the time this plan was released, 92% of all milestones were complete and had been accepted by VITA. Six milestones remain to be completed as part of transition.

Two critical milestones remain to be completed:

1.   Enterprise agency-wide messaging system cutover (90% completed): this milestone represents the migration of 90% of the Commonwealth users to the Enterprise Email system. With completion of this milestone, nearly all Commonwealth personnel will use a secure email system to conduct Commonwealth business. The Enterprise email system, with active, onsite monitoring 24x7, is located at the Chester Data Center with a backup system implemented at the Southwest Virginia Data Center. The backup provides the ability to resume email operations within four hours in case of a prolonged outage of the primary system. After the completion, the legacy systems in operation can be decommissioned, reducing operations and maintenance costs

for Commonwealth agencies while providing improved, reliable service to end users. It is planned to be completed in April of 2010.

2. Complete Agency LAN migration (90% completed): Northrop Grumman already achieved 90% checkpoint with implementation of approved plan to migrate "hot" ports from the legacy Commonwealth networks to the new MPLS network. The completion time for this milestone is January of 2010.

Four other milestones remain to be completed:

1. Information Technology Infrastructure Library (ITIL) Process Optimization: all ITIL workshops completed with representation from Agency IT staff, addressing the ten core ITIL processes. Remaining activities are limited to the Acceptance Test Plan completion and will be completed in April of 2010.

2. Server consolidation complete (90% completed): achieve 90% checkpoint with implementation of approved plan to consolidate 2,341 existing servers across the Commonwealth. October 2009 is the deadline for this milestone.

3. Completion of Desktop Refresh (90% completed): achieve 90% checkpoint with implementation of approved plan to refresh 64,000 desktops across the Commonwealth. Planned completion: December of 2009.

4. Complete Agency LAN migration (68%). Achieve 68% checkpoint with implementation of approved plan to migrate "hot" ports from the legacy Commonwealth networks to the new MPLS network. Planned completion: November of 2009.

At the time of the release of the Corrective Action Plan, the Integrated Master Schedule contained more than 90,000 discrete activities with more than 77,000 of them already completed. Northrop Grumman demonstrated how much progress had been made in key transformational activities. Figure 9.6 illustrates the current level of the project in term of completion.

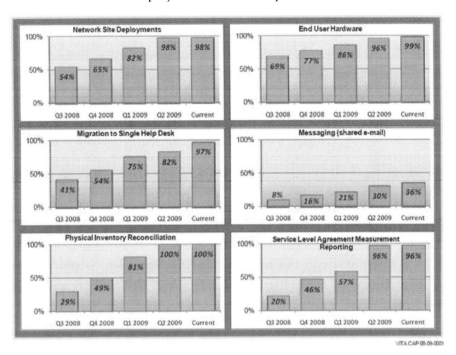

Figure 9.6, Progress Made on Key Transformational Activities

The success of this plan depends on collaboration of Northrop Grumman, VITA and executive agencies. With the reasonable cooperation among these parties, timely completion of all tasks can be achieved. All involved parties must commit to and embrace the management approaches for scheduling, agency coordination, and reporting outlined in this plan. Northrop Grumman has also built 90 calendar days of reserve into its overall schedule to allow for technical and business challenges which reflected lessons learned by all parties to mitigate risks associated with factors not yet identified by Northrop Grumman.

A report dated September 9, 2008, by the General Assembly's investigative arm (JLARC) stated that there were several ongoing issues with inventory, computer equipment replacement, agency level fees for computers, agency level fees for software licenses, customer service, and the IT help desk. While agencies have complained that VITA/NG "rates are excessive; that they would pay less if they still were able to go into the marketplace rather than forced to operate through VITA." JLARC stated this issue "contributes to the tension between 'centralization and agency autonomy.'" In addition, the commission report stated that "agencies have raised concerns about the adequacy of Northrop Grunman services, despite a $270 million investment by the firm." According to JLARC savings for the public may be evident if the contract is extended beyond a decade and perhaps if Northrop Grumman absorbs information technology work for local government as well as public colleges and universities. Judi Ballesteros, a spokeswoman for Northrop Grumman, said in a written statement that the company--its information technology wing will work with the state to "address any issues" (Shapiro, 9/9/2008).

On October 13, 2009, the General Assembly's investigative arm (JLARC) gave its latest snapshot of the state's disputed computer contract with Northrop Grumman. According to Jeff Schapiro, RTD the Joint Legislative Audit and Review Commission report shows that the giant info-tech program has been blocked by delays, rising costs, and political turmoil. It was revealed that "Northrop Grumman lacked the experience to undertake a project of Virginia's scale. Virginia is apparently the first state to move toward a privately managed information technology system." Ashley Colvin, a JLARC analyst, said that the state gave "low priority" to Northrop Grumman's lack of experience in the management of state computer and communication systems of this scale. Because no other state had attempted such an enterprise, there was "no roadmap" for Virginia, he said. Colvin also noted that the State's former computer chief and Virginia's comptroller said in advance of the 10-year, $2.3 billion contract with Northrop Grumman that the contractor offered Virginia "better value" but "more risk."

Northrop Grumman, a California-based defense giant, operates government computer networks for, among others, San Diego County and Indianapolis and surrounding Marion County. According to Schapiro sast week, the Richmond Times-Dispatch obtained an advance copy of the JLARC study and reported that it might be too expensive for the state to sever its relationship with Northrop Grumman. Depending on the circumstances, junking the contract could cost cash-strapped Virginia nearly $400 million plus the undetermined price of fashioning an alternative system (Shapiro, 10/13/2009).

The future of VITA/NG

With delays, cost over-runs, and poor performance, it is obvious that the transition of outsourcing Virginia's state information technology and system needs has been less than stellar. There has been much in-house bickering, finger pointing, misinterpretations and bureaucracy throughout this whole ordeal. These petty occurrences have only compounded the problems troubling Virginia's outsourcing. Though the past and current events have raised many questions about the execution of Virginia's IT strategy, the fact remains that future action needs to be taken to correct past mistakes.

Current CIO, George F. Coulter who replaced Lemuel Stewart Jr., has begun making strides in taking action to change the situation. He has fired and reassigned many senior executives of VITA in an attempt to reduce political turmoil and streamline the agency. Coulter should continue to take actions with streamlining and centralizing VITA in order to make more effective and proper measures in dealing with Northrop Grumman contracting and performance with relation to costs. As Coulter simplifies the organization, he should follow through on his statement for necessary transparency: "We [are] going pretty much to have an open-book approach with Northrop Grumman on costs and information..." (Shapiro, 9/22/09). This way, there should be no ambiguity about the allocation of costs and funds to correct the direction that Virginia outsourcing is going towards. In addition, Coulter should take one-step further, and publish all final conversations and resolutions between VITA and Northrop Grumman. This will allow Virginia citizens to remain updated on the situation on how everything is coming.

Moreover, VITA has had some friction with the agencies that are in the middle of transitioning. VITA claims that state departments "are basically stalling on transformation" (Ress, 9/13/09). Many state departments retort with implications that VITA does a poor job in transition the departments. "Penny J. Baggett, executive director of the Commission for the Arts, complained to the governor's office that VITA officials had misclassified—as spam—e-mails from a federal agency that she relied on for funds" (Ress, 9/13/09). "'VITA seems to know nothing about our wiring cabinet,' a Department of Minority Business Enterprise official complained to the Governor's office on the second day of a phone outage, after seven calls to the help desk" (Ress, 9/13/09). As a result, Department of Health Professions got permission in March to set up a program to track prescriptions outside of the VITA-Northrop Grumman system. Soon after the implementation of the system, a hacker broke into the new system and stole private information.

To rectify these misunderstandings and quell feuding, VITA needs to take measures to become better acquainted with the individual departments for which they are trying to facilitate the outsourcing process. Additional researching of necessary actions and building specifics for current transitioning departments will help VITA to be more knowledgeable in cabinet wiring and e-mail prioritizations. Conversely, state departments in transition need to be more cooperative by working with their assigned VITA aide who will successfully help transition each department. The idea is to work together with understanding. This will most likely increase costs, but will greatly facilitate the outsourcing process to make things uniform.

Next, disputes between Northrop Grumman and VITA have slowed down the process of outsourcing greatly. Northrop Grumman argues that their dependence on VITA to access multiple sites have delayed accurate cost allocation and delays. VITA contends that Northrop Grumman is trying to build a case to renegotiate contract terms in order to gain more money. Regardless of who is right or wrong, neither side is budging from the stance that the other party is to blame.

To resolve this issue, simple steps can be taken, in conjunction with the previous solutions stated. For Northrop Grumman's accusations, Northrop Grumman technology heads for specific state departments should work closely with the VITA employee whose sole job is to understand state departments in transition. That employee will act as a go-between or medium between the outsourcing of Northrop Grumman and the department end user. This way, Northrop Grumman can avoid the bureaucracy with contacting a random VITA official or representative and have a direct contact for that specific department they are allocating costs. For VITA's issue, VITA should provide an incentive provision that will moderately increase the contract payment based on quickness of transition and end-user rating surveys of Northrop Grumman's performance. Northrop Grumman's recent submission calls for a projection completion of June 2010 (Shapiro, 9/22/09).

The State's interest

In 2003, then-Governor Mark Warner believed that Virginia's technology "is not the right way for any major enterprise to operate" (Ress, 9/13/09). Six years later, with a more business-like approach through VITA, it seems that little has changed. Barely half way through the project and the process has proven poor, incurred cost overruns, and experienced setbacks. The payments to Northrop Grumman are capped at $236 million a year, through 2010. With a growing budget crisis and political conflicts, it is in the state's best interest to continue the outsourcing process, despite possible increases in payments. Virginia could very much benefit from a unified information system that will significantly improve efficiency as well as interdepartmental cohesion. Certainly, it is necessary to have an accurate assessment of performance before making any contract changes. The Joint Legislative Audit and Review Commission will be integral in discerning problem areas of costs and spending.

Governor A or Governor B

As Governor Tim Kaine finishes office, many Virginians are left wondering what the new governor-elect will do to remedy the situation. Republican nominee Bob McDonnell believes that "the performance has got to be better. And state agencies have got to be served better...We can't make excuses, and we can't have delays, and we can't have finger-pointing. Those are unacceptable" (Meola, 9/23/09). McDonnell wants to wait until the reports from JLARC have been completed before making any stands of desired changes to the process. McDonnell still believes that the public-private partnerships are a step in the right direction. As a result, he urges for improved performance: "I don't think anybody would disagree that we need more oversight, more accountability and some retooling of our VITA operation...We've got fine public servants there, but I want to see that organization work better and have better performance all the way around" (Meola, 9/23/09).

Democratic nominee Creigh Deeds had a more specific stance on the current situation. He has expressed, along with Governor Tim Kaine, that the VITA chief should report directly to the governor. As of now, VITA's chief is hired and fired by its oversight board, which contains gubernatorial and legislative appointees. He "[believes] in the fundamental premise of VITA, and [he] worked with Mark Warner to bring a business approach to our IT systems, but it's very clear now that [Warner's] original plan...to have a [chief information officer] appointed by the governor and accountable to the executive branch, is the better approach" (Meola, 9/23/09). Deeds appears to focus on having a more hands-on or direct involvement if he were to be elected. Furthermore, Deeds stated that he would have VITA be the first to be audited if he were elected (Meola, 9/23/09).

Presently, as with all political matters, no one is sure what actions either candidate will perform until after the election process is finished. Despite future uncertainty, both candidates agree that changes need to be made, effective actions are forthcoming, and the current situation is intolerable.

10. Nevada DMV - the genesis[*]

The "Welcome to the Department of Motor Vehicles, please take a number and have a seat. Please be prepared to spend your entire day in that seat, your number most likely will not be called for seven to eight hours."

This should have been the announcement made over the intercom at all Nevada Department of Motor Vehicles and Public Safety (DMV) sites beginning September 7, 1999. This date marks the implementation of Project Genesis-Phase II, the installation of an integrated Windows NT based computer application system designed to improve customer service at the DMV. Since the implementation, lines at the DMV have increased from 40 minutes to over 7 hours. Numerous problems that have occurred in the system include:

- Vehicle titles that are printed overnight have blanks where information such as odometer readings should be.

[*] This case was prepared by Becky Solomon under the tutelage of Dr Gurpreet Dhillon.

- Overcharging of registration on vehicles that were purchased between 1984 and 1985—incorrect additional fees ranged from $8.00 to over $100.00.

- Commercial driver's licenses that should have been suspended due to driving under the influence arrests with convictions are noted on the system as "in good standing". The system did not show any of the convictions. (Tahoe.com, September 14, 1999)

In many of the above instances, the problem could have been adjusted by overriding the system and inputting the correct data, unfortunately, when the DMV technician tried to do so, the system would not allow them to override the information.

Background

The purpose of the new system is not to increase lines and upset Nevada residents, but to improve the organizational structure of the DMV in order to be more customer-oriented. The Department of Motor Vehicles is one of the State of Nevada's largest departments, employing almost 2,200 people in 36 offices statewide. This department was created by legislative action on April 1, 1957. The department's responsibilities include enforcing statutes regarding vehicles and watercraft, licensing motor vehicle carriers and is accountable for all functions of the Public Service Commission, the Driver's License division and the Nevada Highway Patrol. The department is organized into the following divisions: motor vehicle, motor carrier, driver's license, Nevada Highway Patrol, gasoline and special tax, administrative services, investigation and training. (DMVPS History)

Currently the DMV handles 131,000 vehicle registration renewals and 10,000 new vehicle registrations a month. It also handles 6,000 new driver's licenses and 30,000 license renewals per month, about 65% of them from Southern Nevada. (LVRJ, September 24, 1999). In order to keep up with the growth in Nevada, a team of individuals including state employees, legislation, consultants and citizens began a study on the status and improvements needed for the division. Named Project Genesis, this reengineering project focuses on customer service. The team noted that from 1970 to 1980 Nevada's population had increased 63%, from 1980 to 1990 it increased 50% and since 1990 it increased over 25%.

The team looked at the current processes and noted that "DMV has evolved to meet the needs of the state and to carry out state and federal responsibilities. Over time those needs and requirement have changed; new statutes have been implemented; programs have been added and, unfortunately, services have become fragmented. From the customers perspective DMV is a confusing maze of processes that are slow, backlogged, labor intensive and separated." (Project Genesis, May 15, 1996) The system is difficult because technicians must access several different systems to obtain information regarding driver and vehicle information. If the information is not in the system, then the technician must leave their station and search for the information on microfiche. Additional steps have been added because the computer systems do not have the functionality to support the existing processes. Technicians record information by hand, copy the documentation and then make a receipt for it. The technician actually figures the registration on the car by use of a calculator. In addition registration, titles, and driver's licenses are treated separately. When a customer comes in the door to register his/her car and change their driver's license, they must stand different lines for each transaction.

There are two separate computer systems at the DMV. They were both designed in the early seventies, each by an individual outside agent. One is equipped to handle the driver's license information, the other deals with registration information. Each system holds much of the same information, and duplication of this information is both costly and difficult to maintain. A customer may change the address on their driver's license, yet their registration is still sent to the old address.

Except for mail in title requests and mail in registration, all transactions must take place at a DMV office. "The customers must come to us. It is expensive for DMV to maintain offices in convenient locations. As the state grows, this will become even more expensive. It is also expensive for customers. Waiting in line is not only irritating, it results in lost earnings when it requires time off from work." (Project Genesis) The team noted that in order to maintain existing levels of service, DMV would need to add 23 new positions a year. By the year 2015 the five new facilities would need to be built in Clark County alone in order to meet the demands of the growing population. Using state demographics, the team noted a cost avoidance of $133 Million in salary savings from 2002 to 2015. The number of new facilities in Clark County would drop from five to one, saving an additional $40 Million between the years 2002 and 2015. A total cost avoidance would be $173 Million. The cost of the Genesis project was figured at $34 Million. The project, they concluded, would pay for itself by the year 2007.

The team met with DMV employees, benchmarked other states' DMV systems, including Oregon (unsuccessful) and California and reviewed information from industry professionals. With the idea of becoming a customer driven organization the team recommended a three-phase plan (Appendix A) to create an integrated system that would allow for efficient customer contact both at the DMV and off site locations.

Phase I - Foundation Phase

During this phase four components were focused on; system development, continuous improvement, organizational change, and change management. Functional requirements for the integrated system were developed. A detailed plan regarding what the integrated system would be required to do was designed. This included the creation of a data model, providing information necessary for the team that would create the program. At this time an implementation schedule was created. Vendor research was conducted for add-on technology.

Phase II- One Stop Customer Service

Phase two builds on the foundation phase. This is the phase that is currently in progress. The base integrated system was designed, developed, and is currently being implemented. This will provide a core system that will be built on in phase three. Kiosks will be implemented. These kiosks will provide information to customers regarding driver's license requirements, registration and title requirements. A phone-processing center will be implemented. Customers will be able to dial a 1-800 number and receive answers to their specific questions. This alleviates the traffic at DMV offices. Integrated Voice Response Unit (IVRU) will be established for inquiry purposes. Furthermore a court interface will be designed. Through an automatic transfer of data, courts will be able to obtain conviction information. Implementation of restructuring has also occurred, as well as employee training.

Phase III- Alternate Service Methods

This phase build on phase II by adding additional technologies, such as digital document imaging, online and phone registration and renewals and renewals by outside vendors such as smog checks.

Implementation

Phase I has been completed. Two consulting firms have been hired to work with the DMV. Deloitte and Touche were hired for 10 million dollars to write the new integrated systems program. BEST consulting was hired to implement the change management program, including designing new training programs to coincide with the new system.

The DMV is currently in phase II. The new integrated program was put online on September 7, 1999, after several delays. The system was supposed to be online as early as June 1999. This Windows based system integrates both driver's license information and registration information. It also has additional useful information that was not available on the old Honeywell legacy system such as smog check results, mail in registration information, organ donor notice, and complete address change history. Now when a customer sits down at a DMV station, that technician will be able to answer each of their questions, without sending them to another line. It is no longer necessary for a technician to leave their station to look up information on Microfiche because the data is now available at the workstation.

Training

Prior to the implementation of the new integrated system, employees needed to be trained. The first step was cross training. Since employees were assigned to one workstation, they only knew how to operate one of the divisions- driver's licenses or vehicle registrations. All 500 technicians had to be trained in the areas that they were not familiar with. This was a formal training class followed up by counter experience. Training began October of 1998 and would continue through August of 1999. Motor Vehicles' press release states that "as DMV employees gain experience in working with new subjects, customers may experience slight delays." (Motor Vehicles, October 14,1998) The Honeywell Legacy System that was in place, used only a keyboard, but due to the fact that the Genesis program would be Windows based employees were also trained on Windows based programs. Employees were involved in a classroom training to learn how to use Windows NT. Employee's computer literacy varied, some had to learn how to use a mouse for the first time. In addition the DMV set up in-house stations so the employees could become familiar with the mouse.

Two employees from each DMV were sent to extensive training on the new system. The training lasted approximately 6 months, they were then known as "wizards". The goal of the wizard is to assist other employees when they have questions regarding the new program. The remainder of the technicians received one eight-hour course on the new system. This training occurred between the months of April and May. The system that the technicians were trained on was not the same system that they would eventually be using, due to the fact that programmers were still in the process of completing the new system. Employees were trained on parts of the program that were still not fully developed. The system contained many bugs at the time, and employees felt that the information they were learning was not useful, due to the fact that it would be altered before they would use it. Employees' handouts did not match the screens that they were practicing on, and they were told that the screens would probably change by the time that the program was released. The technicians learned to operate a different version of the system than what they would be utilizing in their jobs. An analogous situation would be training an individual on Windows XP, and then expecting them to operate Windows 8.1.

Online

DMV repeatedly warned the public to expect delays and to mail in registrations rather than coming to the DMV offices during the training and implementation period. After several postponements, the Genesis system was released. The bugs in the computer system were greater and much complicated than expected. As of October 6, 1999 there have been 1,926 bugs reported, 66% of them are already fixed, stated Ginny Lewis, Deputy Director of the state Department of Motor Vehicles. Currently, technicians are sending in any problems that they have to Carson City. Once they are entered into a database in Carson City, Deloitte and Touche prioritize the bugs and fix the ten most important. This occurs twice a week. The contract with Deloitte and Touche expires on December 7, 1999, so in order for the consultants to adhere to all of the issues, they have requested that all information regarding the bugs be presented to them by November 5, 1999.

Other public agencies, such as law enforcement also use the DMV system. The Henderson Police Department uses dispatch computers to obtain data. Project Genesis changed the dispatch monitor setups. "Officers that radioed information requests would get only a partial response, such as a vehicle's year or model, or just plain gibberish," explained Sandy Waide, Communications Administrator for the Henderson Police Department's dispatch center. Genesis also caused problems with the Law Enforcement Message Switch system (LEMS). The LEMS serves as a hub for all state and nationwide law enforcement computer systems.

In August, the backlog of mail in registration at the DMV was only one week, as of the first week in October the backlog was five weeks. The lines have shortened from over 7 hours to 4-6 hours, depending on the time of day a customer visits the DMV. On October 8, 1999, Governor Kenny Guinn announced a five-point plan to alleviate the current long lines and back logs at the DMV. The plan consists of:

- A Declaration of Emergency to Hire 42 Temporary Staff-These staff will be trained and assigned to the Renew by Mail or phone department in Carson City.

- 24-Hour Operation of Mail-In Service- The above staff will be working around the clock.

- A 30-Day Grace Period for Registration Renewals- This applies only to those who have mailed in their renewal or have unsuccessfully tried to renew their registration. It does not apply to new registrations or those who have not attempted to renew.

- A Statewide Telephone Hotline for DMV Questions- The hotline can be used to check the status of renewals or to answer simple questions.

- Faster Implementation of New Technologies-The DMV will tackle improvements in customer service during this fiscal year, rather than over the next two years (Phase III). Included are registration renewals at emissions inspection stations and transactions by telephone and the Internet.

Problems

The major issue that the DMV is facing is backlog of information. This is dominant in both the mail in registration division and in at the actual DMV sites, as noted by the long lines. Several important steps need to be looked at in order to see how the backlog transpired to the current unacceptable position.

The problems that occurred during implementation created a chain effect. One of the problems is noted in May of 1999, when the Ways and Means committee rejected the plea from the department for 50 additional new employees. Assemblywoman Chris Giunchigliani said her committee learned that as of April 1999, 83 positions were vacant, in addition 17 jobs that were created in 1997 were never filled. These positions were not filled due to the hiring freeze that was imposed by the past Governor Bob Miller during that time. (LV Sun, May 3, 1999) The necessary hiring of additional staff was not completed. This is both due to the fact that the DMV did not fill current openings and that legislation did not approve of the hiring of additional temporary staff. Legislation noted the obvious facts that the DMV had openings that it could have filled, but chose not to. The procrastination of the DMV backfired when they ultimately realized the need for these individuals at a date that was too late to follow state hiring procedures. The result was understaffing during a period of time when these individuals were most imperative.

Although Legislation was in full support of Project Genesis, but when DMV noted the need for additional employees, legislation did not approve of the temporary hires. This led to another problem: the training of employees. The original cross training of employees began the backlog of lines and mail in registration. This training caused a notable backlog both at the DMV sites and in Carson City. Offices did not hire additional staff to cover for the time that the employees were out of the office in training. In addition, they did not cover the workstations that should have been operational, but were not due to the on the job training in different areas. In situations where there was normally 5-6 employees working the driver's license department, there was only one or two individuals covering while the rest of that department was being trained on registrations.

As additional training continued, each office lacked the two staff members who were sent to become "wizards". This was followed by full office training, which consisted of 2 days training, one day learning Windows, and another day learning Genesis. During this time, no additional temporary staff was used to assist at the DMV offices.

The Genesis training that the technicians were educated on (8hrs) was not compatible with the system that they would be using once online. This caused much confusion. The system had too many bugs at the time of training, so comprehension of the material was difficult for employees, and even if comprehension did occur, employees would not be using the system in the same manner as they were shown.

Conclusion

The implementation of a new system is time consuming and cumbersome. It should be noted that Project Genesis was implemented within budget. Due to the organizational structure of the DMV and the fact that it is a public agency, many political forces were behind implementation. Taxpayers need to be shown that that the money was spent properly and a system was created. The on time implementation backfired. If the project had been delayed, costs in the long run would be less. Currently the State has to pay for additional overtime of regular DMV employees, and the contracting of the 42 temporary staff as well as other aspects of Guinn's 5-point plan.

With the implementation of the high potential project there was much oversight regarding the effects on other agencies. For example, law enforcement, received no training regarding the use of the Genesis program. In addition to this oversight, the use of consultants, Deloitte and Touche and BEST to both create and integrate the new system may have been a mistake. Neither of these consultants had any experience dealing with a DMV system, and to amplify the situation, Deloitte and Touche are still in control of prioritizing the bugs, ultimately deciding the order in which the program will be corrected. In addition, the State had previous difficulties with Best, suing them for a previous project regarding the Taxation department (LVRJ, October 1,1999), yet is willing to pay BEST an additional 600,000 to help remedy the situation. The DMV project will be over budget and the need for hiring additional individuals has increased. Meanwhile, lines are still hours long and backlog of information is continuing to cause customers to receive registration documentation in an untimely manner. The project that was created to assist in customer service issues has done exactly the opposite.

11. Spa Select IT Implementation

After attending an executive steering committee meeting, the message was made clear by The Palm Resort and Club President, Steve Hoffler, that they must receive the Mobil four star during Mobil's next visit to "The Palm." The CFO, Henry Chandler, immediately thought of the Spa and Salon. Chandler knew that the service in this area was lacking, and believed it was primarily due to the lack of guest history and inability of receptionists to track paperwork effectively. This had been an area that Chandler had wanted to address for the past year, however the project was continuously put off. Now more than ever he needed to be sure that this did not become the reason why the property did not receive the four star, and have Hoffler come down on him for not implementing the system long ago. Chandler had decided this weak point in the hotel's IS infrastructure had gone on long enough and informed the CIO, Mike Atkins, that the Spa Select System was to be operational in the Spa and Salon in two months.

The Spa and Salon, although very closely related, were under two different management teams. A well-known hairstylist out of Los Angeles who had experience styling many Hollywood actors managed the Salon. Raymond Philips traveled between Las

Vegas and Los Angeles, where he managed his own studio and typically spent ten days out of the month at The Palm. The Assistant Manager of the Salon came to The Palm as part of the agreement with Philips. Aurora travels between the two locations as well to add coverage on an additional five days per month. As is the case with a majority of the employees working in the Salon, neither manager nor the technicians have any computer experience. The stereotype of the Salon in the past has been one of a free spirited, "artsy" group of people who do not adapt to change well and want to be left alone to concentrate on as one technician put it "the art of hairstyling." The Salon currently runs on a manual system, which has done an effective job of handling the business demand, although there is definite room for improvement.

The Spa is in a similar situation in that the management team does not have any computer experience and has been running on a manual system for the past ten years. Structurally the Spa has gone through some changes over the years. The Spa, when opened ten years ago, had two different positions that worked to serve the guest. Spa Porter's responsibilities were to ensure that towels, products and the juice bar were stocked. They were also responsible for cleaning the lounge, bathroom, showers, sauna, etc. throughout the day. The Spa Attendants served more of a guest relations capacity to the customers. They gave guest tours and directions on the facilities and answered any questions they may have. Spa Attendants handled checking guests in and out, along with coordinating masseuse and estheticians appointments once the guest had arrived. These positions and responsibilities changed under the direction of a previous Spa Manager, who believed that one position should be over these duties, creating more of a team atmosphere. The Spa Porters were then promoted to Spa Attendants and the job descriptions were combined. This created a few challenges for the Spa initially, due to some language barriers and professionalism when handling guests, however this improved relatively fast.

For the Spa, running a manual system had caused more problems than in the Salon. Due to the volume in the Spa, the manual system had caused numerous complaints in tracking guests effectively throughout their stay at The Palm. This included loosing guest-billing slips, difficulty tracking money transactions, and challenges identifying guest's preferences due to a lack of guest history.

Current Situation

The Spa and Salon both use manual systems for their day to day operations. Guests are handed "passports" that they carry throughout their stay in the Spa and Salon. This paperwork becomes cumbersome and would get misplaced when receptionists are closing out the day. The appearance of the desk was also a concern, with multiple pages to flip through to find a guests reservation, this made the desk appear cluttered and unorganized. This situation did not give the guest the impression that the operation was well run or did it present a relaxing, stress free atmosphere that was desired. Under the manual system accounting also had to spend numerous hours adding up and backtracking information, since the manual system created no opportunities for reporting capabilities.

The Spa manual system created a larger struggle from the standpoint of balancing and accounting at end of day. The Spa volume consistently exceeded 450 guests in a day, which created exhorbant amounts of paperwork and an unacceptable time frame to close out, typically taking over an hour to balance a cashier at the end of the day. The receptionists were easily frustrated trying to track down guest paperwork at the different stations throughout the spa if guests were trying to check out. These issues would be non-existent with the new system. All information would be held in the computer and could be viewed from any terminal.

The Salon, on the other hand, was accustom to a different business flow and guest volume, making it possible for them to operate relatively smooth on the manual system. There were still issues with not having guest history and the appearance of the reception desk, but from the receptionist and technicians standpoint the operation ran smooth the way the manual system performed. Tracking issues of guest paperwork was not a concern in the Salon due to the reduced volume as compared to the Spa.

The IS system selection process was simple. The vendor that was chosen was Spa Select Systems. Select Systems is known for the Spa portion of the program and have begun to fine-tune the Salon functionality as the demand has increased for a system that will handle both Spa and Salon in an effort to reduce the number of operating systems in the industry. There were still enhancements that needed to be made to establish the Salon side as user friendly as the Spa functionality, however the system was currently running in multiple operations in the area, including one of the resorts sister properties with no problem. The Paradise Bay Resort and Club had reported some concerns with the Salon side however the vendor was attentive to the needs and concerns and were in the process of working on the enhancements. This made the decision to go with the Select Systems simple, since other properties had not reported any significant issues with the program.

Select Systems International was created in 1990, when a spa owner in California wanted to develop a high-end integrated suite of Windows based software for high volume spa resorts. The end result was a system that was developed for not only spa operations, but retail and food and beverage outlets as well. The Select Systems hospitality suite has the capability of addressing operational needs in food and beverage point of sale, retail point of sale, spa and salon membership and accounting. All modules can be used as stand-alone systems or in any combination to provide an integrated suite of software. An appealing benefit for The Palm Resort to use their system was due to two core competencies of the company. These are product development and client training and installation. Select had proven its track record on the install and opening of The Paradise Bay Resort, since there were little problems with the initial go-live or any serious issues soon there after.

Business Plan Identification

Due to the stringent time-lines on the project there were two people brought in to assist with the implementation of the system. The Corporate IS Lead Analyst, Seth Sanders, and The Palm assigned Projects Manager, Robert Lewis. Sanders and Lewis knew this project would be difficult to pull off due to the time constraints, however they both had worked on system implementations before and were confident they could successfully complete the conversion. The vendor had established a relationship with Sanders due to the implementation at the Paradise Bay Resort and he knew they had a reputation of being thorough and completing system implementations on time.

Following the Vice-President of Hotel Operations meeting with the Salon and Spa Managers Sanders and Lewis toured the Spa and Salon and identified the requirements of the facility and determined where the critical areas were to establish points of contact. Sanders identified where network connectivity was needed and if any engineering requests would be required in order to hold both the PCs and printers. After sitting down with both managers and numerous employees Lewis flowcharted the process (see appendix). He realized there would need to be a modification of the job descriptions in order for the process to run as efficiently as possible. This was due to the fact that the Spa

Attendants could now make reservations, not just check in and check out guests, which increase the efficiency of all employees.

The scale of this project consisted of nineteen contact points and 107 staff members from both the Spa and Salon. Typically for a project this size, Select Systems would send three support staff members for the configuration stage and would reduce that figure to two for training and implementation. The short notice did not give Select Systems the ability to staff properly creating a staffing level inadequate to be complete in their work and training. To add to the time challenges, there were employees that had never used a computer before. This would add to the expected time in training for those who did not have computer experience. To make the situation even more desperate for the implementation team, there were a few employees who were not well versed in the English language. What once was a job that required little writing ability as Spa porters now had transitioned into a job that required them to enter guests into the system and edit spa and salon services.

The property project leaders sat down and established a project timeline for the process. They could not establish a realistic timeline for the project. The hardware was ordered and expected to be in on time, with the exception of bar code scanners for retail items. However due to the departments overall computer illiteracy it seemed unlikely at this point that the implementation would be as smooth as originally hoped. Due to management's complete intimidation of computers Lewis had found himself doing much of the managers responsibilities since neither one was computer literate. Both managers resisted the project and were discouraged by the thought of having to depend on a computer as part of their daily function. The Salon Manager removed himself from all aspects of the system planing sessions, identifying his Assistant Manager as the contact person.

This continued for a week, with Sanders and Lewis preparing most of the information necessary for when Select Support arrived in a week. Lewis began to get concerned as things did not improve and sent an e-mail to the Vice-President of Hotel Operations to document the process and challenges that were being faced. This was done to identify areas that must be addressed before Select Support arrives and to identify items on the timeline that had fallen short of the completed goal date. By doing this, both Sanders and Lewis removed themselves from the firing line if the department heads did not address basic issues that could only be addressed by management.

Planning

After establishing the timeline for configuration, hardware and network testing, training and go-live, Select Systems team members arrived on property for the initial phase of the project, configuration. Select Systems knew what to expect from the managers and staff, do to the conversations with Sanders prior to their arrival, however it was not anticipated that both the Salon Manager and Assistant Manager would be in San Diego. Prior to leaving, the Salon Assistant Manager welcomed the Select support team to configure the system for her and left a number where she could be reached if any questions arose. They were not expected to return for two days which would get them severely behind in the configuration process. The Spa Manager had struggled up to this point to get the necessary information for configuration and was not interested in Salon issues. She had made it very clear that Sanders and Lewis would have to manage the Salon situation alone.

Sanders and Lewis spoke with the Spa Select Support team and the decision was made to create a copy of the Paradise Bay Resort's database and copy the information into the system for the Salon. This would curve the problem faced if configuration was not concluded prior to Salon training. Upon the return of

Raymond and his assistant there was still no sense of urgency to work on the project. Simple items such as billing paper had not even been ordered for the new system yet which Lewis had to order to ensure the Salon had supplies for go-live. The Salon management relied on implementation experts to handle the process for the Salon, knowing that it was there reputation if the project was not successful. Aurora, the Spa Assistant Manager started configuration two days prior to the scheduled training date. With the assistance of Select Support and the Paradise Bay Resort download, she was able to get the system configured the night before training began.

Training

Training began two weeks before the scheduled go-live date. This was not a significant amount of time due to the illiteracy of staff, both of the English language and of computers. Some employees adapted to the computer environment very well, however others in the same class did not know how to use a mouse or in some cases how to spell key words. Training became a discovery and learning session where trainers from Select could not help all of the people because employees did not catch on quickly. Employees with more computer experience were put in situations were they had to assist teaching those that were slower, due to the lack of trainers on property. Credit card transactions and room charges could not be simulated in the test environment since the system was not interfaced with the test property management system, herein called "PMS" Host system. The process was simple, however due to the extensive training and the concerns with adapting; all system scenarios needed to be walked through in advance to ensure that employees understood the process.

Managers also had difficulties with training and grasping the new system. No one understood why the system was installed or why it was needed, which resulted in conflict and challenging of the functionality of the system. Due to the difficulties and frustration that was experienced during training, especially on the part of those not computer literate, one of the Assistant Mangers and two employees quit from the spa. This created further issues due to the fact that there was now a shortage of staff for the preparation of go-live. The Spa Manager was now down four employees and only one week away from the implementation date. Training proceeded as scheduled; it became obvious that something had to be done to get another trainer in, due to the difficulties that were had in getting some of the employees up to speed. Lewis went to the Vice-President of Hotel Operations and advised her of how the training was progressing. It was recommended that an attempt be made to get another person in from Select Systems to assist with training. At this point it was obvious that the one person they did have on property, Jacki Stewart, was not going to be able to handle the additional training that would be required. Jacki was already working seven, twelve-hour days and could not handle the additional training demands. After the Vice-President approved the additional person, Lewis called Sanders to see if anyone had come available from Select to assist with the training. Sergio Flores was sent from Select to meet the additional training requirements and help with go-live. Both Sanders and Lewis felt that at this point they had done everything they could to get the employees trained with the time constraints they were under. It was now up to the managers to keep the employees motivated and get them prepared the rest of the week for go-live on Monday.

Sanders turned his attention back to ensuring the hardware and software were ready for Monday, while Lewis went to meet with the department heads to evaluate how their spirits were and to talk to employees to get a feeling on how comfortable people were with the system. Because of Lewis's concern that someone might sabotage the project, he wanted to make sure that all employees had signed and agreed that they did not need any more training while the opportunity was there. The Spa and the Salon were very sensitive areas in that both were very high profile, servicing not only guests but executives as well. Many of the top executives go to the Spa or get their hair done at the salon, such as the CEO's and President's wives. Employees talking about not receiving enough training or discussing system problems could cause the project to be viewed as a failure and make both Sanders and Lewis look bad. After Lewis spoke with both departments it seemed as though everyone felt okay with the system and were just eager for go live. Raymond Philips and Aurora had still not been trained on the system two days prior to go live. Lewis questioned them both on it and they stated that they had no intentions of learning the system and that the receptionists knew it and would do fine on their own. Aurora knew how to configure, but she did not know the operational side of the system. This posed a large concern for Lewis, since the two managers could not look things up in Spa Select. This made it impossible for them to handle guest complaints or discrepancies since they did not have the know how to maneuver through the screens or to look up a reservation.

Implementation

Sanders was working on the system and configuring the interface of Spa Select to the PMS system. The Palm was the first property the interface had been installed, so there were concerns that there may be some bugs to work out. Sanders seemed confident that everything would go smooth with the interface, so this was not a concern. All computers, printers, and software were in place and ready for go-live, Lewis sat back and reflected on the past two weeks, reviewing the timeline, and flowcharts to ensure nothing was overlooked.

When Monday, go-live day arrived, everything was set up and in working order. The only hardware not in place were the scanners, however everyone was aware that the scanners would not be available. To remedy this situation Select System was temporarily configured so that employees could enter the bar code manually.

Select support had two people made available to the Spa and Salon, in addition to Sanders and Lewis to help assist with the system and any questions that may arise. The Spa Manager was also present, however the Salon Manager and Assistant Manager were not in town. They had gone to San Diego and were not expected back for two days. The Salon handled the transition well, with some issues in regards to waiting, since the receptionists and attendants were not familiar with the system. These problems were to be expected during any normal implementation and were expected to be smoothed out over the next few days. Problems were experienced with reservations missing in the system and not being able to find lost reservations. After looking into this complaint and other similar issues it was identified that a majority of these problems were derived from human error. Employees insisted that Spa Select was changing locations of services and that they were entering the information correctly. Other issues also arose, such as poor customer service. This was nothing that hadn't been dealt with in the past when implementing a system. Lewis and Sanders had spoken to the Spa Manager earlier in the day and advised her that any problems or complaints that were received should be comped off, no questions asked. This was standard policy whenever implementing a new system and was considered part of implementation cost. Overall, the supporting staff was pleased with how the first day was panning out on the new system for the Spa. The remaining managers had really worked hard to get everyone trained the best they could with the time constraints, taking directions to do whatever necessary to ensure her staff was ready for go-live.

The Salon however was in another situation. There was very little communication between management, the receptionists, and the technicians who perform services for the guest, whether it be nails, feet, or hair. Technicians were accustom to the manual system where the receptionists would manually rotate customers to be sure that all technicians received an equal amount of business. This was crucial since technicians in the Salon are paid on straight commission. The staff in the Salon were not comfortable enough on the system to shuffle day of appointments around to distribute the customers evenly between the technicians. This caused the entire staff to be angered by not receiving appointments they were accustom to getting, based on seniority. Because of this, the receptionist were now dealing with guests, and mad employees on the first day of implementation. To make matters worse, no one from management was available since both the Salon manager and assistant manager went to San Diego. Technicians were advising executives including the President and his wife about problems that they were having with the system and with the entire implementation process. This was putting everyone on guard; instead of concentrating on the issues at hand, everyone was ensuring they had covered themselves before moving on to other tasks. Lewis was getting calls from Chandler and the Vice-President of Hotel Operations attempting to find out specifics on incidences the President had heard from employees while getting salon services.

Lewis and Stewart from Spa Select were left with no choice but to attempt to resolve the situation with the disgruntled employees. After hearing what their concerns were and what problems they were having, it seemed obvious that some of the issues were due to user error, however employee's salaries could not be sacrificed due to these problems and lack of training. Under the manual system the guests were scheduled to technicians by seniority. If a client canceled, the receptionist would erase the clients and shuffle them around to ensure that the highest seniority would get the first customer. Select, as mentioned previously was intended for a spa system initially and was being configured and enhanced to handle the Salon end more effectively. This being the case, Select was not capable of making this adjustment. The Palm Salon rotation as configured in Spa Select primarily by seniority and second, on a point scale. The configuration was set up so that people who have worked at The Palm from ten to eight years have top seniority, seven to five have next seniority, and so on. Within these seniority groups appointments are given out to the person with the least amount of points, until everyone in the group have an appointment booked. The following is an example of how the system books appointments:

On a day where no appointments are booked, the system would give the first appointment to a person in the highest seniority group (This is done alphabetically by group). Once the system has assigned an appointment to all people in the highest seniority group, Select will then give one appointment to all of the technicians in the second level, and so on. Once every stylist has received an appointment the system will then start over giving the next appointment to the people in the highest seniority group. At this stage Spa Select will assign the appointment to the technician with the least points in that group. The system does not calculate requests into the number of appointments booked. If a technician has an appointment that cancels the next appointment booked goes to that person (Unless the tech is already booked during the requested time).

Lewis looked to the Paradise Club Salon for direction as far as how they handle the rotation issue. They rotated so that the person with the lowest dollar value booked that day receives the next appointment. This was the only restriction, appointments were not juggled from one person to another for seniority reasons and everyone was given an equal number of services.

After discussions with Stewart about this issue, Lewis devised an alternative to assist those using the system so they could "manually" move appointments effectively by knowing who has the lowest "points." The following is what Stewart and Lewis agreed would work after completing an enhancement on the system.

The proposal was to book clients similar to how Paradise Club handles their rotation with the exception of requests for technicians. This was the technician's way of increasing their paycheck, by providing good customer service and relying on repeat business. Identifying and booking requests for technicians independently from the rotation. By not including these requests in the points total per technician this promotes, good customer service, strong skills in their respective areas, and most importantly, will improve on the over-all guest experience.

All other appointments would be booked on a point system, based on dollar value. Technicians who once relied on seniority to boost their earnings would now have to rely on good customer service and requests to achieve a higher dollar value than their peers since the earnings between technicians should be relatively flat with the exception of requests.

Lastly an enhancement was made to show the total number of points each technician has to facilitate smooth transitions when moving clients to other technicians. This alternative puts the focus back where it needs to be, on the clients as opposed to the technicians and encourages good customer service, which has always been the number one priority of The Palm. It seemed obvious that the technicians were attempting to sabotage the system, since they did not understand the value created or how it could benefit them. The situation only escalated when management was not available to assist with dealing with employee issues.

Property Management System Interface

After the first day of operating on the system, Sanders, Lewis and the Select Support team went to dinner to discuss the days activities and what needed to be done to improve the situation. Numerous discussions were had on the issues in the Salon and the aggravation surrounding the lack of supervision in that area. The interface was brought up in the conversation and concerns arose that this was never checked once the system went live. Sanders assured everyone that this was not a problem and that the interface was working properly the day before when it was tested. The discussion that followed was concerning posting codes. This was another area that Sanders felt confident in, although Lewis knew this was something he had over looked. He knew that Sanders had extensive IS background but not operations and that he should have been involved in this part of the interface setup. The following day Lewis ran test folios to ensure that there were no problems with the interface. After pulling up the folios in the PMS system, Lewis realized that the posting codes were wrong and that the interface had to be brought down to fix this. Although a fix such as this does not typically take an extensive period of time, remotely taking an interface down could cause other issues to result. Sanders agreed to take the interface down to make the corrections and Lewis ran more test folios to verify they were correct.

Conclusion

Following this incident, Sanders began pulling himself away from the project. Lewis knew he only had two days left with the trainers. The Salon Manager still had not returned from San Diego, but were expected the following day. Lewis, expected to be in the Salon for a while until the receptionists could handle the system on their own. To attempt to facilitate a faster transition Lewis began to write policies for the system and how to run required reports, close out at the end of the day, balance, etc. He also began writing the policies for City Ledger account charging, cross-property charging room charging, etc. Although Lewis knew the implementation did not go as well as it could have, he was pleased with the results when considering the time allowed and other difficulties. Lewis just hoped that Raymond Philips and the Assistant Salon manager, Aurora would be proactive in heading off the concerns of the employees when they returned.

Considering the challenges faced with the Spa and Salon management and employees, I believe that Lewis, Sanders, and the Select support team made the best of a bad situation. This is an obvious case of resistance to change and a fear of the unknown. When the managers heard computer, they did not care what the benefits would be, since they were intimidated by the thought of using computers.

With a lot of assistance, the Spa manager made it through the transition and worked to adapt to the IT implementation. One negative aspect of this situation was that she was so caught up in her own concerns that she forgot to properly address her employees. This resulted in some of them leaving since they were as scared as she was.

The Salon Manager, on the other hand, took an opposite initiative. He turned his back and never was interested. This showed as an end result in his employees who had fought the system, the rotation, and all other aspects of the Select System, stating that it was inadequate in all aspects as it relates to their job. Salon technicians did not want the system so they demanded unrealistic expectations of it, as indicated by their requests for system rotation. Reflecting back on this implementation there were many areas that improvements could have been made.

Appendix 1

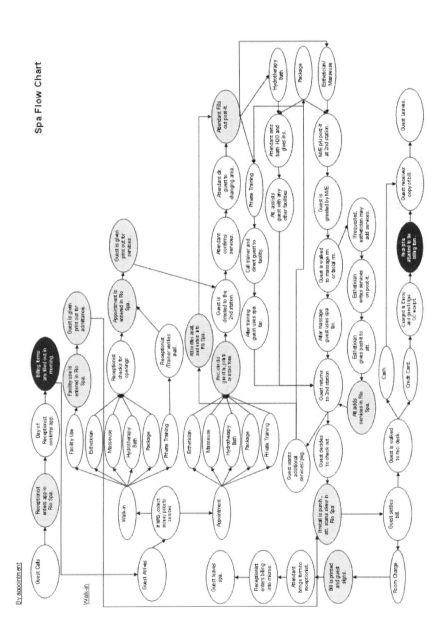

Spa Flow Chart

Appendix 2

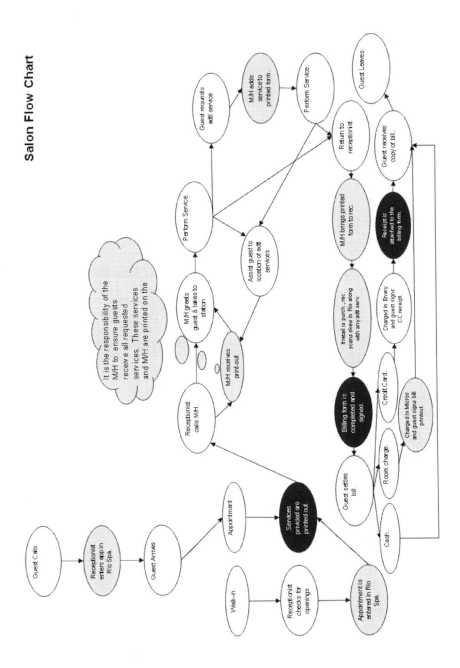

References

Ali, A. (1996). Pioneering Versus Incremental Innovation: Review and Research Propositions. The Journal of Product Innovation Management 11(1): 46-61.

Amabile, T.M. (1983). The social psychology of creativity, Springer-Verlag, New York.

Andrews, K.R., (1971) The Concept of Corporate Management, Irwin, Homewood Il.

Angell, I.O. (1996) Economic crime: beyond good and evil. Journal of Financial Regulation and Compliance, 4(1).

Angell, I.O. (2000) The new barbarian manifesto: how to survive the information age? London: Kogan Page.

Ansoff, H.I., (1965) Corporate Strategy, McGraw Hill, New York.

Anthony, R., (1965) Planning and Control Systems: A Framework for Analysis, Harvard University, Boston, MA.

Antonoaie, C., and Antonoaie, N. (2010). Computer-based simulations. Bulletin of the Transilvania University of Braşov. Vol, 3, 52.

Aversano, L., Canfora, G., Aniello, C., & De Lucia, A. D. (2002). Migrating Legacy Systems to the Web: an Experience Report. Benevento, Italy.

Bacque, P. (2008) Outsourcing of Va.'s IT system hits snags, The Richmond-Times Dispatch, December 14.

Barney, J. B. (1997) Gaining and Sustaining Competitive Advantage. Reading, MA: Addison-Wesley Publishing Company

Bartlett, C. A., and Ghoshal, S. (1989) Managing across Borders: The Transnational Solution. Harvard Business School Press

Barlett, C. A., & Ghoshal, S. (1989). Matrix management: not a structure, a frame of mind. Harvard business review, 68(4), 138-145.

Barua, A, Konana, P., Whinston, A.B., Yin, F. (2004) An empirical investigation of net-enabled business value. MIS Quarterly, 28 (4): 585-620. 31(2).

Basu, V., et al., The impact of organizational commitment, senior management involvement, and team involvement on strategic information systems planning. Information & Management, 2002. 39: p. 513–524.

Benjamin, R. I. and Levinson, E., (1993) A framework for managing IT-enabled change, Sloan Management Review, Summer, pp. 23-33.

Benjamin, R.I. and Levinson E., (1993) A framework for managing IT-enabled change. Sloan Management Review, p. 23-33.

Bianchi, A., Caivano, D., Marengo, & Visaggio, G. (2003). Iterative Reengineering of Legacy Systems. Barti, Italy.

Boehm, B.W., et al., (1978) Characteristics of software quality. Amsterdam: North Holland.

Bowen, J., (2000) The ethics of safety-critical systems. Communications of the ACM, 43(4): p. 91-97.

Brophy, J.T. and Monger, R.F., (1989) Competitive capacity from an integrated IS infrastructure, Information Strategy: The Executive's Journal, 5, 2, pp. 26-33.

Brunsson, N. (1982) The irrationality of action and action rationality: Decisions, ideologies and organizational actions." Journal of Management Studies, 19, 29-44.

Burn, J.M. and Loch, K.D. (2001) The societal impact of the World Wide Web - key challenges for the 21st century. Information Resources Management Journal, 14(4).

Cap Gemini Ernst & Young. (2002). World Class Business Integration & Billing Support. DiToro, L. (2003). BMP and Legacy Systems. Retrieved July 22, 2008, from BMP Enterpirse.com: http://www.bpmenterprise.com/content/c060515a.asp

Carr, A.: (1968) Is Business Bluffing Ethical? Harvard Business Review (January/February).

Carson, T. L.: (1993) Second Thoughts about Bluffing, Journal of Business Ethics 3(4).

Cash, J.I. and Konsynski, B.R., (1985) IS redraws competitive boundaries, Harvard Business Review, March-April, 1985.

Cecil, J. and Goldstein, M., (1990) Sustaining competitive advantage from IT, The McKinsey Quarterly, 4, pp. 74-89.

Chandler, A.D., (1962) Strategy and Structure in History of the Industrial Enterprise, MIT Press, Cambridge, MA.

Child, J. (1972) Organizational structure, environment and performance: The role of strategic choice. Sociology, 6: 1-22.

Child, J. (1997) Strategic Choice in the analysis of action, structure, organizations and environment: Retrospect and prospect. Organization studies, 18 (1): 43-76.

Ciborra, C. (1993). Teams, markets and systems: business innovation and technology. Cambridge, Cambridge University Press.

Ciborra, C. (1994). Market support systems: theory and practice. Global telecommunications strategies and technological changes. G. Pogorel. Amsterdam, North-Holland: 97-110.

Ciborra, C. and Jelassi, T. (1994) The grass roots of IT and strategy, in Strategic information systems. A European perspective, Wiley: Chichester. p. 3-24.

Ciborra, C., (1994) The grassroots of IT and strategy, in C. Ciborra and T. Jelassi, editors, Strategic Information Systems: A European Perspective, John Wiley & Sons, Ltd, Chichester, pp. 3-24.

Clemons, E.K. and Weber, B.W. (1991) Information technology and the changing nature of the financial services industry, in Collaborative work, social communications and information systems, R.K. Stamper, et al., Editors, Elsevier Science Publishers: Amsterdam. p. 93-116.

Conner, K.R. and Rumelt, R.P. (1991) Software piracy: an analysis of protection strategies. Management Science, 37(2): p. 125-139.

Crescenzi, A. D. (1988), The dark side of strategic IS implementation, Information Strategy: The Executive Journal, 5, 1.

Croall, H. (1992) White collar crime. Milton Keynes, UK: Open University Press.

Daugherty, Patricia J., Matthew B. Myers, and Chad W. Autry (1999), "Automatic Replenishment Programs: An Empirical Examination," Journal of Business Logistics, Vol. 20, No. 2, pp. 63-82.

Dhillon, G. (2001) Violation of safeguards by trusted personnel and understanding related information security concerns. Computers & Security, 20(2): p. 165-172.

Dhillon, G. (2008). "Organizational competence in harnessing IT: a case study." Information & Management 45(5): 297-303.

Dhillon, G. & Lambert, R. (1996) Organizational competence for harnessing IT: the case of John Brown Engineering. In Proceedings of the First UK Academy for Information Systems Conference, Cranfield School of Management, Cranfield, Bedford, April 10-12

Dhillon, G. and Orton, J.D. (2001)Schizoid Incoherence, Microstrategic Options, and the Strategic Management of New Organizational Forms. Management, 4(4): p. 229-240.

Dhillon, G., Moores, T. and Hackney, R. (2001) The emergence of networked organizations in India: a misalignment of interests? Journal of Global Information Management, 9(1): p. 25-30.

Duffy, D. (1999) A capital idea, in CIO.

Earl, M. (1996) Information systems strategy ...why planning techniques are not the answer. Business Strategy Review, 7(1): p. 54-67.

Earl, M. J. (1990). Approaches to strategic information systems planning experience in twenty-one United Kingdom companies. Eleventh International Conference on Information Systems, Copenhagen, Denmark.

Earl, M., (1989) Management Strategies for Information Technology, Prentice-Hall, Hemel Hempstead.

Earl, M., (1992) Putting IT in its place: a polemic for the nineties, Journal of Information Technology, 7, 1992, pp. 100-108.

Earl, M., (1993) Experiences in Strategic Information Systems Planning, MIS Quarterly, March, pp. 1-24.

Earl, M., (1996) Information systems strategy ...why planning techniques are not the answer, Business Strategy Review, 7, 1, pp. 54-67.

Earl, M.J. (1989) IT and strategic advantage - a framework of frameworks, in Information Management - the strategic dimension, M.J. Earl, Editor. Oxford University Press: Oxford. p. 33-53.

Earl, M.J. (1993) Experiences in strategic information systems planning. MIS Quarterly, p. 1-24.

Earl, M.J. (1994) Knowledge as strategy: Skandia International, in Strategic information systems: a European perspective, edited by C. Ciborra and T. Jelassi John Wiley: Chichester.

Elgesem, D. (1996) Freedom of expression and the regulation of Internet access in academia. in 3rd International conference on values and social responsibilities of computer science (ETHICOMP96). Madrid, Spain, November: Universidad Complutense de Madrid.

Esther Gal-Or & Anindya Ghose, (2005) The Economic Incentives for Sharing Security Information, Industrial Organization 0503004, EconWPA.

Estrin, D. (1987) Interconnection of private networks, Telecommunication Policy, September, 247-258.

Falkenberg, G. (2006, October 1). New Legacy Modernization Strategies and Disciplines. Darmstadt, Germany.

Financial Times. www.ft.com. Archives Search on Business Name.

Floyd, S. W. and Woolridge B., (1990) Competitive strategy, IT and performance, Journal of Management Information Systems, 7, 1, pp. 27-44.

Flynn, D.J. and Goleniewska, E., (1993) A survey of the use of strategic information systems planning approaches in UK organisations, Journal of Strategic Information Systems, 2, 4, pp. 292-319.

Foster, R. N. (1986). Innovation: The Attacker's Advantage. New York, Summit.

Galbraith, J. R. (2010). The multi-dimensional and reconfigurable organization. Organizational Dynamics, 39(2), 115-125.

Gale Research, Inc. (1995) Market Share Reporter, 5th edition. From LEXIS/NEXIS research.

Galliers, R. (1987). Information systems planning in a competitive strategy framework. Information management, state of the art report. P. Griffiths. Maidenhead, Berks, Pergamon Infotech.

Galliers, R.D., (1991) Strategic information systems planning: myth, reality and guidelines for successful implementation, European Journal of Information Systems, 1, 1, pp. 55-64.

Geen, R. G. (1991) Social motivation, Annual Review of Psychology, 42, pp. 377-400.

Gluck, F.W., Kaufmann, S.P. and Walleck, A.S. (1980) Strategic management for competitive advantage. Harvard Business Review

Gordon, Lawrence A. & Loeb, Martin P. & Lucyshyn, William, (2003) Sharing information on computer systems security: An economic analysis, Journal of Accounting and Public Policy, Elsevier, vol. 22(6), pages 461-485.

Gottschalk, P. (1999) Implementation predictors of strategic information systems plans. Information & Management, 36: p. 77-91.

Greenwood, R., and Hinings. C.R. (1988) Organization design types, tracks, and the dynamics of strategic change. Organization Science, 9, 293-296.

Hambrick, D.C., Finkelstein, S. (1987) Managerial discretion A bridge between polar views on organizations. In LL Cummings and Barry M. Staw (eds), Research in Organizational Behavior, 9: 369-406; Greenwich, CT: JAI Press.

Hamel, G. (1996) Strategy as revolution. Harvard Business Review, p. 69-82.

Hamel, G. and Prahalad, C.K., (1994) Competing for the Future, Harvard Business School Press.

Hammer, M. (1990). Reengineering work: don't automate, obliterate. Harvard Business Review (July-August): 119-131.

Hart, P. J., and Saunders, C. S. (1998) Emerging Electronic Partnerships: Antecedents and Dimensions of EDI Use from the Supplier's Perspective, Journal of Management Information Systems (14:4), pp. 87-111.

Hart, P., and Saunders, C. (1997) Power and Trust: Critical Factors in the Adoption and Use of Electronic Data Interchange,"Organization Science (8:1), pp. 23-42.

Henderson, J. and Sifonis, J.G. (1986) Middle out strategic planning: the value of IS planning to business planning. in The 1986 NYU Symposium on Strategic Uses of Information Technology, New York. NYU.

Henderson, J.C. and Venkatraman, N., (1993) Strategic alignment: leveraging information technology for transforming organisations, IBM Systems Journal, 32, 1, pp. 4-16.

Hinings, C. R., and Greenwood, R. (1988) The Dynamics of Strategic Change. Oxford: Basil Blackwell

Hofer, C.W and Schendel, D., (1978) Strategy Formulation: Analytical Concepts, West Publishing, St Paul, MN.

International Telecommunication Union, World Telecommunication Development Report 1998. ITU: Geneva, Switzerland.

Johnston, H.R. and Carrico, S.R. (1988) Developing capabilities to use information strategically. MIS Quarterly, 12(1): p. 37-48.

Johnston, K. and Yetton P., (1996) Integrating IT divisions in a bank merger: fit, compatibility and models of change, in J D Coelho et al., eds., Proceedings of 4th European Conference on Information Systems, Lisbon, Portugal, July 2-4.

Joint Legislative Audit and Review Commission, (2009) Interim Review of the Virginia Information Technologies Agency, presentation to the Senate Finance Committee, June 29.

Keefe, P. (2004, November 1). Oops! Ford and Oracle mega-software project crumbles. Retrieved 8 5, 2008, from Application Development Trends: http://www.adtmag.com/article.aspx?id=10182

Kishore, R., Sharman, R., and Ramesh, R. (2004) Computational ontologies and information systems: I. Foundations, Communications of the Association for Information Systems, Vol.14 No.8, pp.158-183

Lederer, A.L. and Salmela, H. (1996) Toward a theory of strategic information systems planning. Journal of Strategic Information Systems, 5(3): p. 237-253.

Lederer, A.L. and Sethi, V. (1988) The implementation of strategic information systems planning methodologies. MIS Quarterly, 12(3): p. 445-461.

Lee, Hau L. and Seungjin Whang (1998), Information Sharing in a Supply Chain. Research paper No. 1549. Research Papers Series, Graduate School of Business, Stanford University.

Lee, J. K., Upadhyaya, S., Rao H. R., and Sharman, R. (2005) Secure Knowledge Management and the Semantic Web, Communications of the ACM, Vol.48, No.12, pp. 48-54

Lonnqvist, A. and Mettanen, P. (2002) Criteria of Sound Intellectual Capital Measures. in Proceedings of the 2nd International Workshop on Performance Measurement. Hanover, Germany, June 6 - 7.

Brodie, M and M. Stonebraker, (1995) Migrating legacy systems: gateways, interfaces and the incremental approach, Morgan Kaufman Publishers Inc., San Francisco

Mars, G. (1982) Cheats at work. An anthropology of workplace crime. London: George Allen & Unwin.

Martin, J. (1992)   Cultures in Organizations: Three Perspectives. New York: Oxford University Press,.

Martinez, E.V. (1995) Successful reengineering demands IS/ Business partnerships. Sloan Management Review, p. 51-60.

Martocchio, J.J. (1992) Microcomputer usage as an opportunity: the influence of context in employee training. Personnel Psychology, 45: p. 529.

Mata, F.J., Fuerst, W.L. and Barney, J.B., (1995) Information technology and sustained competitive advantage: a resource based analysis', MIS Quarterly, 19, 4, pp. 487-506.

Mcaffe, A., Dessain, V., & Anders, S. (2006). Zara: IT for Fast Fashion. Harvard Business Review, pp. 1-23.

McCall, J.A. (1979) An introduction to software quality metrics, in Software quality management, J.B. Coper and M.J. Fisher, Editors. PBI: New York.

McFarlan, F.W. (1984) Information Technology changes the way you compete. Harvard Business Review

McGolpin, P. (996) An examination of the inter-related factors and issues affecting the degree of success with strategic information systems: throughout the application lifecycle. PhD Thesis 1996, Cranfield University School of Management: Cranfield, Bedford, UK.

McGrath, R. G, MacMillan, I. C. and Venkataraman, S., (1995). 'Defining and developing competence: a strategic process paradigm', Strategic Management Journal, 16, 4, pp. 251-275.

Meola, Olympia and David Ress. (2009) Disputed Va. IT Bill was paid improperly. Richmond Times Dispatch, July 14.

Meola, Olympia and Jeff E. Shapiro. (2009) E-mails show clash over paying Northrop Grumman. The Richmond Times Dispatch, July 28.

Meola, Olympia. (2009) Va. told that its IT costs could swell, The Richmond Times-Dispatch, July 25.

Meola, Olympia. (2009) McDonnell criticizes information-technology agency. Richmond Times-Dispatch. September 23.

Mills, C.W. (1956) The power elite. Oxford: Oxford University Press.

Miles, R. E., Miles, G., Snow, C. C., Blomqvist, K., & Rocha, H. (2009). The I-form organization. California Management Review, (51).

Mintzberg, H. (1994) The Rise and Fall of Strategic Planning. New York: Prentice Hall

Mintzberg, H. and Waters, J., (1985) Of strategies deliberate and emergent, Strategic Management Journal, pp. 257-272.

Mintzberg, H., (1987) Crafting strategy, Harvard Business Review, July-August, pp. 66-75.

Mintzberg, H., (1990) The design school: reconsidering the basic premise of strategic management, Strategic Management Journal, 11, pp. 171-195.

Montakab, C. (2005). Legacy Transformation. Business Rule Extraction and Transformation of COBOL Applications. London, United Kingdom.

Moores, T. and Dhillon, G. (2000) Software piracy: a view from Hong Kong. Communications of the ACM, 43(12): p. 88-93.

Nah, F. F., Lau, J. L., et al. (2001). Critical factors for successful implementation of enterprise systems. Business Process Management Journal 7(3): 285-296.

Ning, L. and L. Xiwen (2007). Innovation of Complex Technologies: Five Cases, Five Cultures. 5th International Symposium on Management of Technology (ISMOT '07) Hangzhou, China.

Ogilvie, d. and Fabian, F. (1999). Decision making requirements for future organizational leaders: A creative action-based approach. Chapter 4. In James G. (Jerry) Hunt, George E. Dodge, and Leonard Wong (Eds.) Out-of-the-box leadership: Transforming the 21st century Army and other top-performing organizations, JAI Press, Westport, CT.

Ohmae, K. (1995) The end of the nation state. New York: The Free Press.

Okkonen, J. (2002) Performance Measurement in Virtual Environment. in 2nd International Workshop on Performance Measurement, IFIP WG5.7 SIG. Hanover, 6. – 7. June.

Olsen, G; Cutkosky, M; Tenenbaum, J & Gruber, T. (1994) Collaborative Engineering based on Knowledge Sharing Agreements Proceedings of the 1994 ASME Database Symposium, September 11-14, Minneapolis, MN.

Orton, J. D. and Dhillon, G. (2006). Macro-Strategic, Meso-Strategic, and Micro-Strategic Leadership Processes In Loosely Coupled Networks. Sharing Network Leadership. LMX Leadership: The Series – Volume 4. . G. B. Graen and J. A. Graen. Greenwich, CT, Information Age Publishing.

Orton, J. D., and Weick, K. E. (1990) Loosely coupled systems: A reconceptualization. Academy of Management Review, 15, 203-223.

Oster, S. M. (1990) Modern Competitive Analysis, pp. 172-75; 177-81. New York: Oxford University Press.

Peters, T. (1992) Liberation Management. New York: Knopf

Pettigrew, A. and Whipp, R., (1991) Managing Change for Competitive Success, Blackwell Scientific, Oxford.

Pettigrew, A.M., (1985) 'Contextual research: a natural way to link theory and practice', in E.E. Lawler, ed., Doing Research that is Useful in Theory and Practice, Jossey Bass, San Francisco.

Pettigrew, A.M., (1987) Context and action in the transformation of the firm, Journal of Management Studies, 24, 6, pp. 649-670.

Porter, M. (1980) Competitive Strategy. New York: Free Press

Porter, M. (1985) Competitive Advantage. New York: Free Press

Porter, M. and Millar, V. (1985) How information gives you competitive advantage. Harvard Business Review, 63(4): p. 149-161.

Porter, M.E. (1980) Competitive Strategy: Techniques for Analysing Industries and Competitors, Free Press, New York.

Porter, M.E., (1985) Competitive Advantage: Creating and Sustaining Superior Performance, Free Press, New York.

Prahalad, C.K. and Hamel, G., (1990) The core competence of the corporation, Harvard Business Review, pp. 79-93.

Pyburn, P., (1991) Redefining the role of information technology, Business Quarterly, Winter, pp. 89-94.

Quinn, J.B. (1980) Strategies for Change: Logical Incrementalism. Homewood, IL: Irwin

Rahanu, H., Davies, J. and Rogerson, S. (1996) Ethical analysis of software failure cases. in 3rd International conference on values and social responsibilities of computer science (ETHICOMP96). Madrid, Spain, November: Universidad Complutense de Madrid.

Reich, R.B. (1992) The work of nations. New York: Vintage Books.

Ress, David. (2009) Northrop Grumman running late on Va. computer work, The Richmond-Times Dispatch, July 22.

Ress, David. (2009) Unfulfilled promises haunt VITA. Richmond Times-Dispatch. September 13.

Ress, David. (2009) VITA pays contractor $9,000 over life of a laptop, The Richmond-Times Dispatch, July 24.

Roberts, K.H., Stout, S.K. and Halpern, J.J. (1994). Decision dynamics in two high reliability military organizations, Management Science, 40, pp. 614-624.

Sabath, Robert E., Chad W. Autry, and Patricia J. Daugherty (2001), Automatic Replenishment Programs: The Impact of Organizational Structure, Journal of Business Logistics, Vol. 22, No. 1, pp. 91-106.

Salmela, H. and Spilb, T.A.M. (2002) Dynamic and emergent information systems strategy formulation and implementation. International Journal of Information Management, 22: p. 441–460.

Schapiro, Jeff. (2008) IT deal no money saver yet for State. Richmond Times-Dispatch. December 9.

Schapiro, Jeff. (2009) Report Highlights Northrop Grumman's lack of experience. Richmond Times-Dispatch. October 13.

Schapiro, Jeff. (2009) VITA chief wants Northrop Grumman to control costs. Richmond Times-Dispatch. September 22.

Scott Morton, M., e.d., (1991) The Corporation of the 1990s: Information Technology and Organisational Transformation, Oxford University Press, New York.

Senn, J.A., (1992) The myths of strategic systems: what defines true competitive advantage?, Journal of Information Systems Management, Summer, pp. 7-12.

Sharman, R., Kishore, R., and Ramesh, R. (2004) Computational ontologies and information systems: II. Formal Specification. Communications of the Association for Information Systems, Vo.14 No. 9, pp.184-205

Simon, H. A. (1976) Administrative Behavior. 3rd edition. New York: Macmillan

Smith-Jentsch, K.A., et al. (1996) Can pretraining experience explain individual differences in learning? Journal of Applied Psychology, 81(1).

Stalk, G., Evans, P. and Shulman, L.E. (1992) Competing on capabilities: the new rules of corporate strategy, Harvard Business Review, March-April, pp. 57-69.

Steiner, G., (1979) Strategic Planning, Free Press, New York.

Sullivan, C.H. (1985) Systems planning in the information age. Sloan Management Review. Winter.

Susarla . A., Barua, A., Konana, P., Whinston, A. (2004) Operational Impact of Information Sharing between Firms Workshop on Information System and Economics, Maryland.

Swinyard, W., Rinne, H. and Kau, A. (1990) The morality of software piracy: a cross cultural analysis. Journal of Business Ethics, 9(655-664).

Tuomi, I. (2000). Internet, Innovation, and Open Source: Actors in the Network. Association of Internet Researchers Conference. Lawrence, Kansas.

Tushman, M. L. and O'Reilly, C. A. III (2002). Winning through Innovation. Boston, Harvard Business Press.

Tyler, B.B., Steensma, H.K. (1995) Evaluating Technological Collaborative Opportunities: A cognitive modeling perspective. Strategic Management Journal 16: 1995: 43-70.

Ulrich, D., Lake, D. (1990). Organizational Capability: Competing from the Inside Out. New York: John Wiley.

Vitale, M.R. (1986) The growing risks of information systems success. MIS Quarterly, p. 327-334.

Waema, T.M. and Walsham, G., (1990) Information systems strategy formulation, Information Management, No. 18, pp, 29-39.

Wagner, E. and S. Scott (2003). Networks, negotiations and new times: The implementation of enterprise resource planning into an academic administration. Information and Organization 13(4): 285-313.

Ward, J. and Griffiths, P. (1996) Strategic planning for information systems. Chichester: Wiley.

Warren, M. and Hutchinson, W. (2001) Cyber terrorism and the contemporary corporation, in Information security management: global challenges in the new millennium, G. Dhillon, Editor. Idea Group Publishing: Hershey. p. 53-64.

Weckert, J. (1996) Intellectual property rights and computer software. in 3rd International conference on values and social responsibilities of computer science (ETHICOMP96). Madrid, Spain, November: Universidad Complutense de Madrid.

Weick, K.E. (1984) Small wins: Redefining the scale of social problems. American Psychologist, 39, 40-49.

Wernerfelt, B., (1984) A resource-based view of the firm, Strategic Management Journal, 5, 2, pp. 171-180.

Willcocks, L. and Lester, S., (1993) Evaluation and Control of IS Investments: Recent UK Survey Evidence, Oxford Institute of Information Management, Templeton College, Oxford, RDP93/3, Research and discussion paper.

Wood-Harper, A.T., et al. (1996) How we profess: the ethical systems analyst. Communications of the ACM, 39(3): p. 69-77.

Zou, Y., & Kontogiannis, K. (2003). Reengineering Legacy Systems Towards Web Environments. Waterloo, Ontario, Canada.

About the Author

Dr. Gurpreet Dhillon is Professor of Information Systems in the School of Business, Virginia Commonwealth University, Richmond, USA. He holds a Ph.D. from the London School of Economics and Political Science, UK. His research interests include management of information security, ethical and legal implications of information technology. His research has been published in several journals including *Journal of Management Information Systems, Information Systems Research, Decision Support Systems, European Journal of Information Systems, Information Systems Journal Information & Management, Communications of the ACM, Computers & Security, and International Journal of Information Management* among others. Gurpreet has authored several books including *Principles of Information Systems Security: text and cases* (John Wiley, 2007). He is also the Editor-in-Chief of the *Journal of Information System Security*. Gurpreet's research has been featured in various academic and commercial publications and his expert comments have appeared in the *Knowledge@Wharton, New York Times, USA Today, Business Week, NBC News*, NPR among others. He has also been extensively quoted in the International media, including *CNN-IBN, Hindu, Times of India, Hindustan Times, The Tribune*. In 2013 Gurpreet also published his first poetry book – *The Inner Truth*.

Made in the USA
Lexington, KY
11 May 2015